THE WIDOWS OF CLYTH

Plays by the same author:

THE JESUIT

SOMERVILLE THE SOLDIER

The Widows of Clyth

A PLAY BY

DONALD CAMPBELL

PAUL HARRIS PUBLISHING

EDINBURGH

First published
by PAUL HARRIS PUBLISHING
25 London Street, Edinburgh
1979

Cased ISBN 904505 79 0
Paper ISBN 0 904505 80 4

Published with the financial assistance of the Scottish Arts Council

Printed in Scotland
by THE SHETLAND TIMES LTD
Lerwick, Shetland

INTRODUCTION

On Wednesday, the twenty-sixth of January, 1876, six men from Clyth, in Caithness, put out to sea to fish for haddock. Their names were: David Sutherland, Thomas Sutherland, William Sutherland, Robert Sutherland, Donald Sinclair and William MacKay. The following morning, almost within sight of their own homes, the boat was wrecked and they were all lost. Between them, they left behind five widows and twenty-six children in a state of acute poverty.

What follows is concerned with the aftermath of this tragedy and its intention is to be both hypothesis and metaphor. On the one hand, I have tried, by gathering together fragments of fact, folklore and oral tradition, to be as accurate as possible in the representation of events: on the other, by reaching for dramatic insights of a more universal application, I have been forced to include some elements of fiction in the narrative. This has led to a number of unavoidable inaccuracies and I can only hope that those who are familiar with the situation will understand and forgive my licence.

A word or two needs to be said about the language. Since the very distinctive Caithness dialect would usually create considerable problems for actors and audiences alike, I have avoided its use, preferring instead to incorporate Caithness idioms in the written English of the text. Few dialect words are used and, except where absolutely necessary — e.g. 'Weeck' for Wick — no dialect spelling at all. Several well-known Scots usages (notably the preposition 'til') have been employed, and preponderance given to the second person singular 'ye' (pronounced with a long 'e') rather than the more usual plural 'you'. My hope is that actors who know Caithness speech will be able to exploit their knowledge, while those who do not have this capacity will not feel encumbered by the text. While enjoining actors to pronounce my words as they see fit, I must add the strongest qualification that, *on no account whatsoever,* must a conventional 'Highland' accent ever be used in any performance of this play.

DONALD CAMPBELL
Edinburgh, March 1979

for Janie

CHARACTERS

The Sutherland Widows:

> **BETSY**
>
> **HELEN**
>
> **ANNIE**
>
> **CHRISSIE**
>
> **KEET**

The Men:

> **HECTOR SUTHERLAND**
>
> **GEORGE CLYNE**
>
> **MARKIE BREMNER**

The play is in two acts. The first is set in January, 1876, the second ten years later, in August 1886.

ACT ONE

SCENE ONE

The scene is a crofter's cottage in Caithness in the late evening of the 27th January, 1876. The focal point of the room is the hearth — to the right of centre on the stage — a range fireplace with mantlepiece and hooks in the chimney. A long wooden kist and a rocking chair sit on the right-hand side of this, while on the left there is a smaller armchair, a creel for the peats and a small stool. A pot and a kettle of water sit on the hob. To the right of the hearth, there is a double bed, to the left a long table and chairs. Behind this, against the wall, there is a dresser with china sitting on its shelves. A stone jug of whisky sits on the dresser and there is an empty bucket on the floor beside it. Entrance is obtained by a door which stands between the dresser and the hearth. An additional exit is obtained behind the bed. The sound of wind and sea can always be heard, faintly but quite definitely, in the background. As the action begins, HECTOR SUTHERLAND, *a handsome, well-built young man in his middle twenties, is discovered seated on a chair next to the table. Dressed in oilskin jacket, gansey and sea-boots, he is obviously distressed, leaning forward, elbows on knees, head in hands. He looks up, sits up, stretches himself in the chair and gives a long sigh. He proceeds to voice his thoughts with a quiet intensity.*

HECTOR How do ye live with the dead? When the end comes a door closes fast and there is never a road back til the living. *(Nods.)* We know that much in our cradles! *(Rises.)* The trouble is — there are so many doors! How do we find one

9

and other afterwards? How do we live with the dead? *(Takes a few steps towards the bed.)* This man was my brother, he taught me all that I know. The little things as well as the big, the things that matter, the things that are only for fun! How to tie my lace and how to bait a line, how to win a fight *(smiles)* and how to sing a song! But he's taken a road now that he can never teach me to follow. Oh, how can I live with the dead? *(Shakes his head.)* The minister likely has an answer. *(Quotes.)* 'In my father's house there are many mansions' — maybe too many. *(Nods and turns away from the bed.)* As sure as death, we say — but there's none can be sure of what follows after. All the certainties are with the living. All certainty and all hope. If the day comes that they find myself — as I found him this day — what hope will there be for me? What hope for a man that the ocean has taken, cast back on the rocks of his native shore, the strength shaken from his body and the light dead and wasted in his eyes? *(Shakes his head.)* There's no road back for the dead!

He freezes into a short silence — to be broken abruptly by an anguished series of screams from off-stage.

HELEN *(off, screaming)* Thomas! Thomas! Oh, my Thomas!
BETSY *(off, anxiously)* Helen, now . . .
HELEN *(off, uncontrolled)* Thomas! Oh, Thomas!
BETSY *(off, cajoling)* Comeaye, Helen! Comeaye intil the house! We'll see till it, I promise ye . . .
HELEN *(still screaming)* No! No! Leave me alone! Thomas! I want my Thomas!
BETSY *(off)* Oh, steady, lassie, steady now! *(Sharply.)* Keet! What do ye be standing there for, gaping like a bairn? Can ye no see the state ye're sister's in? Give me a hand with her, will ye no? *(Firmly.)* Now, Helen, comeaye in when I tell ye!

Enter BETSY, HELEN *and* KEET. BETSY *is a woman in her mid-thirties, tall and strong-featured.* HELEN *is about ten years younger, of slighter build and possibly more feminine in appearance.* KEET *is barely twenty, a pretty girl but with the gaucherie and innocence of youth. All are dressed in traditional peasant clothes, with shawls over their heads.* BETSY *and* HELEN *wear mutches to denote their married status, while* KEET *is bare-headed under her shawl.* HELEN *is very distressed and is weeping and struggling with the other two.*

BETSY   That's it, Keetty, keep a good grip on her! *(To* HELEN.*)* Comeaye in and calm yourself, Helen, afore ye go any further! Take a droppie broth and . . .
HELEN   Broth? Ye keep your broth. I'll need to go til my man . . .

HELEN *tries to go out again.* BETSY *bars her way.*

BETSY *(warningly)*   Now, Helen!
HELEN *(angrily)*   Och, ye! Get out of my road!

HELEN *tries to struggle past* BETSY, *who restrains her. Watched helplessly by* HECTOR *and* KEET, *they struggle for a moment before* BETSY, *her temper leaving her, pushes* HELEN *away from her and delivers a smart slap across* HELEN'S *face. This stuns* HELEN *for a moment. Angrily, she raises her arm to retaliate, but* BETSY *steps forward, raising a warning finger to* HELEN'S *face.*

BETSY   Dare ye? Dare ye? *(Sharply, with a degree of contempt.)* For the love of the Lord, woman, take a grip on yourself!

HELEN *slowly crumples. She drops her head into her hands and weeps pitifully.* BETSY *takes her shoulders tenderly and draws her into a warm embrace.*

BETSY *(with compassion)*   That's it, lassie, that's it. Let it all run out of ye — let it all go! *(Looks up at* HECTOR.*)* Hector?
HECTOR   Aye, Betsy?
BETSY   Finish the job ye started, boy. Go ye now with Keet and

11

bring Thomas Sutherland til the warmth and comfort of his own bed.

HECTOR *(nods)* Aye!

HECTOR *moves to the door.* KEET, *concerned and bemused by the whole scene, seems reluctant to go.*

KEET Betsy, do ye no want me til . . .

BETSY *(gently, but firmly)* Do as I tell ye, Keetty!

HECTOR *takes* KEET *gently by the arm and leads her out.*

HECTOR Come on with me, Keet.

Exit HECTOR *and* KEET.

BETSY Now, Helen! Comeaye ye and sit down here! *(*HELEN *allows* BETSY *to lead her to the armchair, where she sits down.)* There ye are now! What will ye take? A droppie broth — or maybe a dram would be better?

HELEN *shakes her head sadly.*

HELEN No, Betsy. Nothing.

BETSY Ye're sure?

HELEN *(nods)* Oh Betty, I'm sorry! I didna mean to make such a show of myself — with Hector there and all!

BETSY *(dismissively)* Och, Helen . . .

HELEN *(with difficulty)* It was only . . . seeing him . . . lying there on the cart . . . with his eyes open, staring at nothing . . . his great body stiff and cold and still . . . *(Breaks down again.)* Oh, Thomas, Thomas! My Thomas!

As HELEN *starts to sob,* BETSY *claps her hands together and, attempting brightness, moves briskly to the dresser.*

BETSY That settles it! We'll take a dram! If ye're no needing

12

it to steady your nerves, I'm surely needing it to steady mine!

BETSY *takes two cups from the dresser and picks up the whisky jug. She uncorks it and pours out two stiff measures.*

BETSY   I'm no sure what this'll be like, mind ye! Geordie Fraser only brought it by yesterday and David hasna . . . *(Hesitates as she speaks her husband's name, then shrugs.)* Well, I don't know, of course, but they always say ye can swear by Geordie Fraser! *(She puts down the jug, picks up the cups and moves back to* HELEN.*)* Well, here ye are then, Helen. If nothing else, it'll warm ye up at least!

HELEN *takes the whisky reluctantly.*

HELEN   Honestly, Betsy, I . . .
BETSY *(imperiously)*   Drink it, woman!

HELEN *sips at the whisky and shudders.* BETSY *moves to the rocking chair and sits down.*

HELEN   Oh, Betsy! How did this happen? How *could* it happen?

BETSY *takes a drink before answering.*

BETSY *(in gentle reproof)*   Och, Helen! Be honest with yourself, woman!
HELEN   Honest? How d'ye mean?
BETSY   He was at the sea, was he no? It was always likely, ye surely knew that?
HELEN *(shakes her head)*   No! No him! No my Thomas; *(Quickly takes another drink of whisky and rises, calmer, and walks a few steps downstage).* I'm no sure if I can explain it or no, but from the very first moment I . . . *(Turns to* BETSY *eagerly.)* Oh, Betsy, do ye mind? (BETSY *nods in understanding.* HELEN *turns sadly away once more.)* I never thought — I honestly never thought that there was a power on earth could

hurt him! *(Tearfully.)* He was such a mountain of a man!

BETSY *(with a sad, reminiscent smile)* Aye! Goliath! A fine, big man, Thomas!

HELEN And he never cared for the sea, Betsy! Ye know that yourself!

BETSY *(nodding)* Aye.

HELEN Often he'd say til me that he longed to be quit of it! *(Pauses uncertainly.)* The thing is, Betsy, I knew.

BETSY Eh?

HELEN I knew it was going to happen! Oh, I had a feeling anyway — a presentiment, a sensation, call it what ye like! *(Nods.)* This morning, when they werena home, I knew I'd never see Thomas again in this life . . .

HELEN *starts to weep again. Surprised at* HELEN'S *admission,* BETSY *lays her cup down on the kist and goes to her.*

BETSY Helen . . .

Enter KEET, *followed by* HECTOR, *bearing the dead body of* THOMAS, *wrapped in a sheet. At the sight of them,* HELEN *begins to lose control and takes a step towards them.*

HELEN Oh, Thomas!

BETSY *moves quickly to intercept* HELEN, *putting her arms round her and taking her to one side.*

BETSY Steady now, Helen, steady! *(Jerks her head urgently at* HECTOR *and* KEET, *who have paused momentarily at* HELEN'S *advance. They exit quickly to the right.)* Ye'll have to try to be brave, lassie! Now, finish your whisky, will ye? Comeaye! *(*HELEN *drinks.)* That's it! Right then — are ye ready? *(*HELEN *draws herself up and nods.)* I'll tell ye what we'll do. *(Takes the cup from* HELEN.*)* Ye and me, we'll go through there evennow and see til Thomas. We'll get the wet clothes off him and wash him and dress him up proper.

14

BETSY *moves away from* HELEN, *taking the empty cup to the dresser.*

HELEN *(hesitantly)* Betsy — ye're no thinking there's more to follow, are ye?

BETSY, *taken by surprise, turns quickly.*

BETSY What's that?

HELEN *turns to face her.*

HELEN Your David and Annie's Beel and Chrissie's Robert — Maggie's Donald and Keet's Willie?

Enter HECTOR *and* KEET. BETSY *glances towards them, noticing that* KEET *looks alarmed.* HELEN *ignores them, pursuing* BETSY.

HELEN They're no all gone like Thomas, have they? They've no all perished on the ocean?

BETSY *hesitates for a second, then puts the cup down on the dresser in a dismissive gesture.*

BETSY Likely no.
HELEN Oh, Betsy . . .

BETSY *turns on her sharply.*

BETSY No, Helen! No, no, no! *(Approaches her.)* Likely they've been blown off course a bittie, that's all! *(To* HECTOR, *with a warning glare.)* What d'ye think, Hector?
HECTOR *(taking his cue)* Ach, they'll have put in at Weeck, as like as no!
BETSY *(to* HELEN*)* Ye see? *(To* HECTOR.*)* That'll be Thomas in now, is it?

HECTOR *nods.*

15

BETSY Fine ye are, then! *(Takes* HELEN'S *arm.)* Comeaye now, Helen . . .

Sadly but deliberately, HELEN *removes* BETSY'S *hand.*

HELEN No, Bets! *(Smiles.)* He was my man and this is for me to do — on my own, if ye please.
BETSY *(doubtfully)* If ye're sure ye'll manage?
HELEN *(nods)* I'll manage.
BETSY *(conceding)* Well, then . . .

Exit HELEN, *watched silently by the others.*

KEET *(attempting brightness)* Well! Will I warm up a droppie of broth?
BETSY *(smiling to* HECTOR*)* Hector has the look on him for something stronger, I'm thinking!
HECTOR *(protesting wearily)* No, no, Betsy — no me! Broth'll suit me grand!
BETSY Well, just as ye like, boy! *(Indicates the armchair for* HECTOR *to sit down.)* Stick the pottie on, Keet — I'll see if there's a scone. Ye'll take a scone, Hector?
HECTOR Oh, surely, Betsy!

HECTOR *sits down as* KEET *hooks the pot up at the fire.* BETSY *goes to the dresser and takes down three bowls.*

KEET Hector was saying there's no sign of the boat, Betsy.
BETSY *(absently)* What's that?
HECTOR The boat, Betsy! The *Inflexible.* There's no sign of her!
BETSY Oh! D'ye tell me that, now?
KEET That's something, surely! I mean, if there was a wreck . . .

BETSY *takes the bowls over to the hearth and hands them to* KEET.

16

BETSY Here, Keetty, set that down til warm, will ye? And see me that cup! (KEET *takes the bowls from her and hands her the cup from the kist.*) And how've ye been getting on, Hector? We've no seen much of ye this whiley past!

HECTOR *(politely)* Och, just the usual, Betsy. I've been in Weeck for the past month or so, of course — working with Donnie Morrison until the new boat was ready.

BETSY *returns to the dresser, takes out a napkin of flour scones, a dish of butter and a plate.*

BETSY Donnie Morrison? Oh aye, I mind him fine. And how's Donnie doing, Hector? Weeck suiting him yet, is it?

HECTOR Oh, hardly that, Betsy! He's been speaking of moving on for a while now!

BETSY *goes to the table with the scones and butter.*

BETSY Moving on, is it? Where's he off til, then?

HECTOR New Zealand, he says.

BETSY New Zealand! *(Returns to the dresser and takes out a knife.)* Lord bless me, that's an awful road! He's surely never feared!

KEET, *who has been watching the broth, turns from the fire.*

KEET Where d'ye think they've got til, Hector? Are ye quite certain it'll be Weeck?

HECTOR Och, I canna be sure, Keet. I've heard tell of boats being blown as far north as Shetland afore this!

KEET *(amazed)* Shetland! Betsy, did ye hear that?

BETSY *is buttering* HECTOR'S *scone.*

BETSY *(without much enthusiasm)* Aye, I heard. *(Turns to hand the plate to* HECTOR.*)* Here ye are, boy. Try a bite of that!

HECTOR Thank ye kindly, Betsy.

HECTOR *takes the plate and begins to eat the scone.*

17

BETSY   Keet, is that broth no warmed yet?

KEET *gives the pot a look.*

KEET   Barely. *(To* HECTOR.*)* Hector, when will we know?
HECTOR *(mouth full)*   Know what?
KEET   Know about our men, of course! Whether or no they're
all safe! How long will we have to wait?

Not knowing what to say, HECTOR *turns hopelessly to* BETSY.

BETSY *(sharply)*   Until they come home, Keetty — that's how
long! *(Indicates the pot.)* Now watch ye what ye're doing with
that pot — afore ye burn the backside out of it altogether!
(Pulls back a chair from the table and turns to HECTOR *conversationally.)* And ye've no notion for New Zealand yourself,
have ye, Hector?

HECTOR *lays his plate down on the stool.*

HECTOR   No, Betsy — no me.
BETSY *(smiling)*   Settled as ye are, is it?

KEET *takes a cloth and moves the pot from the hook back on
to the hob. Kneeling in front of the fire, she tastes the soup
with the ladle.*

HECTOR   Och, I don't know, Betsy. Often I'll take a thought
for the Merchant Navy, but . . . well I've the *Dauntless,* my
new boat. She's well run in now and the fishing's no so bad.
(Sighs.) Then there's my mother to think of!
BETSY   Ah Aye! Grannie Ellen would miss ye surely! She'd no
like ye running off til New Zealand.
KEET   That's the broth ready.
BETSY *(irritably)*   Well, put it out, lassie, put it out!

BETSY'S *acerbity is getting to* KEET. *She takes a deep breath and begins to ladle the broth into the bowls.* BETSY *rises and goes to the rocking chair.* KEET *hands the first bowl to* HECTOR, *who accepts it with a smile.*

HECTOR *(smiling)* Thank ye, Keetty. I'll no pretend I'm no ready for this!

BETSY *(as she sits down)* Aye, ye'll have had a hard night of it yourself, Hector! A hard night and a long day!

HECTOR Och, it's no been so bad, Betsy. We've come through worse. *(Takes a sip of the broth, hesitates.)* I saw the *Inflexible* this morning, ye know — as I was coming in.

KEET *(eagerly)* Did ye now?

HECTOR *(nods)* She was til my starboard at the Skerry — I'm sure it was her anyway. *(Pauses unhappily.)* I could see Thomas, standing up in the owse-room, baling with the shovel.

KEET Did ye see Willie?

Slightly stung by KEET'S *insensitivity to his distress,* HECTOR *hesitates.*

HECTOR No! No, Keet, I didna see Willie. As I say, it was hardly more than a look. But it was the *Inflexible* all right, ye can take my word for that. There wasna a bigger man in all Caithness than Thomas, my brother.

KEET Hector, what d'ye think happened? I mean, how did Thomas . . .

HECTOR *(painfully)* Oh, he'd be pitched overboard, likely! It'd be easy done in weather like thon!

Insensitive to his pain, KEET *pursues him.*

KEET But, if that was the case, how could they no . . .

BETSY *(abruptly)* Keetty, will ye get on with that broth, afore it gets cold all over again!

KEET *throws* BETSY *a resentful glance, which is returned by a warning one from* BETSY. KEET *ladles out two bowls of broth, passes one to* BETSY, *then turns once more to* HECTOR.

19

KEET If they were at your back, Hector, how was it that they'd no come in behind ye?

HECTOR *smiles ruefully, rises, vacating the armchair for* KEET, *who slips into it as* HECTOR *moves to the table.*

HECTOR David's the canny man, Keet. I got myself into a bit of trouble at the Skerry, ye see . . .

BETSY Trouble, Hector?

HECTOR *(with a sigh)* My own fault, Betsy. *(Grimaces.)* I was just a wee bit too cocky. I forgot all about the mother wave.

KEET *(uncomprehending)* The mother wave?

BETSY I think that's the first wave, Keet, the one that starts all the others off. That's it, Hector, is it no?

HECTOR *(nods)* Aye! The mother wave! *(Half-chuckles.)* The daft thing is, thon's normally a good sign for fishermen! Often enough, ye'll be coming home on a foggy morning with no hope of a clear sight of land. That's when ye look for the mother wave — it's a big swell and ye can see it from far out in the ocean. It's always close to land — so ye know then the road to run.

HECTOR *finishes his broth.*

KEET What happened, Hector? Tell us!

HECTOR *puts his empty bowl on the table with a smile, takes a deep breath and starts to explain.*

HECTOR It was all wild steering coming in — in weather like thon, it's hardly possible to steer by compass — and I didna have a right idea of where we were. To tell ye the truth, we were lucky to get away at all afore the big seas broke! *(Nods with pride, speaks half to himself.)* The *Dauntless* was foaming at the bows a bittie as we got under weigh — but once she had a bit of sail on her, how she flew! And she needed to fly and all — we could tell that the weather was coming and we

20

needed to get home afore it came down proper. When the big seas came, we ran them at the tails — we were flying through them from first til last! *(Shakes his head with a degree of pride.)* The light was poor as we came in. I could tell we were near til land, but I couldna see the lie of it. I knew where we were — because of the Skerry — but I couldna see the landing. So I brought the wind abeam — to get the mast and the sails out of the road — and that's when I saw the *Inflexible*. As we came round, I got a look til the seaward — and there she was.

BETSY Are ye certain, Hector? Are ye certain it was her?

HECTOR I told ye, Betsy. I saw Thomas. *(Pauses before going on.)* But it was just a look. The very next minute, the mother wave broke til my port and near capsized me! The tail of the wave struck her from the mast aft, and she lay down til it, sail and all! Every room in her — forby the run, where we had the fish — every room in her was full of water, the whole boat was submerged! I lost sight of the other lads and I thought for a minute . . .

KEET *(breathlessly)* What did ye do, Hecter?

HECTOR What could I do, Keetty? I just kept her going, that's all — gave her sail and more sail. *(Nods, with eyes closed, remembering.)* Just held on tight and kept going! *(Smiles.)* Then, the surge broke, the sail dropped and, all of a sudden, it was like running through a field of snow. We were home.

There is a small silence as he ends his tale.

BETSY Aye! And David would see all this, would he?

HECTOR Well, Betsy, if I could see him, he'd surely see me — but he'd no be able to make out whether I'd made the shore of it or no! If I know my brother David, he'd no be eager to come in if he thought there was a chance of a capsized vessel fouling his course. He's far too canny for that, is David.

KEET But what else could he do?

HECTOR The weather was blowing from south til east — he'd run afore it, hope to make a safe anchorage.

KEET But what if he couldna?

BETSY *(irritably)* Och, Keet!

KEET *(snapping at* BETSY*)* Well, Thomas didna find a safe anchorage, did he?

BETSY *gives an anxious glance towards the other part of the house.*

BETSY *(angrily)* Wheesht, lassie!

KEET *(in a low voice, with clenched teeth)* Well, he didna, did he?

HECTOR *(quietly)* What happened til Thomas might have happened til anybody, Keet. If a man goes overboard in a sea like thon, there's never a chance of stopping for him.

KEET *(not to be outdone)* Well, then! If what ye say is true — and they've made for the north, for Weeck — how is it that ye found Thomas miles til the south?

BETSY The sea does funny things, Keet.

HECTOR *(assenting)* Aye!

KEET *rises, concerned. She goes to the table and puts down her bowl.*

KEET I don't know. *(Turns on them.)* I don't know how ye can both be so calm about this!

BETSY Lord bless me, lassie, how else are we to be about it? *(*KEET *looks surprised.)* D'ye think we've no been through all this afore now — dozens of times? *(Laughs.)* Fegs, Keetty, if I was to worry myself sick every time David was late home from the sea, I'd be in my grave afore this!

KEET *approaches her, addressing her in a low, angry voice.*

KEET Betsy, Thomas is dead! Afore long, he *will* be in his grave! *(Pauses.)* And all the rest of them are a whole day nearly late in coming home!

BETSY Och, a day's nothing, Keet! Ye wait for nine days without word afore ye worry — is that no right, Hector? *(HECTOR nods and* BETSY *rises, goes to the table and puts down her bowl. She turns to* KEET, *approaching her kindly.)* Now listen ye here til me, Keetty. If ye're to be a fisherman's wife, lassie . . .

KEET *turns on her angrily.*

KEET   I'm no a lassie! No any more! *(Spitefully.)* And I'm as much a fisherman's wife now as I'll ever be! *(*BETSY *starts suspiciously as* KEET *turns away, close to tears.)* This morning, when they werena home, I felt a cold and lonely shiver come all over me . . . *(Shakes her head.)* I'm no thinking I'll ever see Willie again in this life. I'm no thinking we'll ever be married properly.

BETSY *(severely)*   Huh! Maybe it's as well!

KEET *(surprised)*   Eh?

BETSY   It's far too early in the day to be thinking thoughts like thon! Ye'll be devil the bit of good til Willie if ye'll give up on him this easy!

KEET *begins to retort, changes her mind with a dismissive sigh.*

KEET   Och, Betsy! I'm no a fool altogether, ye know! Ye like to treat me as if I was, but I'm no! I'll no put a brave face on what I know to be true!

HECTOR *(intervening)*   But it's no true, Keetty — no yet, anyway! *(Pauses, offering comfort.)* Listen, Geordie Clyne's off til Weeck with the cart. He'll be back shortly and ye never know who he'll bring with him!

KEET *refuses comfort. She shakes her head and makes no reply.*

BETSY   Hector, I'd take it as an obligement from ye if ye'd go up the road a bittie and watch out for George.

HECTOR *is puzzled by this, but agrees.*

HECTOR   All right — if ye like!

HECTOR *gives a last, concerned glance in* KEET'S *direction and exits. When he has gone,* BETSY *turns sternly to* KEET.

BETSY   Now then, Keet — what's all this about ye never getting married properly?

KEET   I'll never be married in the kirk — in front of the minister.

BETSY *(coldly)*   Is there any other way to be married?

KEET *(sulkily)*   Ye know what I mean.

KEET *begins to move away from* BETSY, *who seizes her by the shoulder and turns her back.*

BETSY *(angrily)*   No, Keetty — I do *not* know! I'm waiting for ye to tell me!

KEET *knocks her hand away angrily.*

KEET   I'm feared, that's all! Anything wrong with that?

BETSY   Depends on what ye're feared of!

KEET   Saturday was to be my wedding day — I'm feared it'll never come!

BETSY *(sarcastically)*   Oh, Saturday'll be here all right, Keet! Ye can depend on that!

KEET *(angry and frustrated)*   Och, ye! Ye needna make fun of me!

BETSY   I'll stop making fun of ye when ye stop telling me lies and tell me the truth!

KEET   I've told ye the truth, have I no? *(Tearfully.)* I'm feared that Willie's been lost and 'll no come back till me!

BETSY   Oh, I see! Ye've set your heart on being a bride on Saturday and poor Willie'll just spoil it all for ye if he goes and gets himself drowned at sea — is that it? *(As* KEET *reacts*

24

angrily, BETSY *drops her sarcasm and shakes her head.)* No, Keetty. That's no the lassie I know. There's something more intil this — something ye're no telling me.

KEET *(coldly)* And how would ye know that?

BETSY Because I know ye. Because ye're my sister. Because I've tended til ye and looked out for ye ever since ye were in the cradle! *(More kindly.)* Now, comeaye Keet! What is it. Ye can tell me, can ye no?

Weary with argument, still unsure of herself, KEET *sits down on the armchair.*

KEET Och, Betsy! It might be nothing . . .

BETSY Maybe it is — but I'll no know until ye tell me!

KEET I'm no sure ye'll understand. Ye see, Willie and me . . . well, there's never been any question but that we were to be married and . . . well, I never thought and . . . *(unable to find the words, she looks up at Betsy and blurts it out)* . . . Betsy, I think I'm going to have a bairn!

In spite of her confirmed suspicion, BETSY *is momentarily taken aback.*

BETSY Oh! *(Recovers.)* Oh, is that all? *(Puts her hand on* KEET'S *shoulder.)* Well, that'll be nice for ye, will it no?

KEET *rises anxiously, gripping* BETSY'S *hands.*

KEET But, Betsy . . . if Willie's gone and we canna marry, that'll mean my bairn's a . . .

BETSY *takes* KEET *in a rough, comforting embrace.*

BETSY Oh, Keetty, Keetty, Keetty! *(Holds* KEET *by the shoulders at arm's length.)* How often do I have to tell ye, woman? Wait afore ye worry!

KEET *breaks from her and turns away.*

KEET I canna help it, Betsy! It's the waiting that makes me worry!

BETSY Oh, Keet! *(Pauses, thinks.)* Look, the first thing is, it's far from likely that the boats been wrecked. Though I do say so myself, my David's the finest skipper on this coast — and he's come through far worse weather than they had last night.

KEET I know that, but . . .

BETSY And the second thing is, even if there has been a wreck — which God forbid! — there's two lads aboard her that'll have a better chance than any of the others. Your Willie and Donald Sinclair.

KEET *(puzzled)* How?

BETSY Well, they're both of them great for the swimming, are they no? That Donald Sinclair, they're saying he's the greatest swimmer in Scotland! And your Willie's no far off being as good!

KEET Aye, but . . .

BETSY *(sadly, half to herself)* My David could never swim a lick! *(Brightening, to* KEET.*)* Still, often he'll joke about it! 'Never heed about me, Bets!' he'll say. 'If we ever get intil trouble on the ocean, Donald'll just hoist me on his back and swim til America!' *(Laughs.)* Ye see, Keet, there's every chance that the boys'll win home safe!

KEET *(still worried)* But what if it's too far for them to swim?

BETSY But what if it's no? Oh, look on the bright side, Keetty! There's Hector just done telling us that he sighted the *Inflexible* no far off land!

KEET *(with relief)* Aye, that's right!

BETSY Ye see? And ye can trust my David to keep them as close til the shore as he dares, if he thinks they'll have to swim for it! *(Pauses.)* Keet, the time for ye to worry about your wedding and your bairn'll maybe come soon enough — but it's no here yet! What ye should be worrying about evennow is . . .

Enter HECTOR, *hurriedly.*

26

HECTOR   Betsy, there's a light on the road! I think it must be Geordie coming home.

KEET *(anxiously)*   Oh, Betsy . . .

BETSY *(soothing)*   Now, just keep ye calm, Keet. Keep ye calm.

Enter HELEN, *carrying a bundle of Thomas's clothes. Pre-occupied with her own thoughts as she enters, she immediately realises that something has happened.*

HELEN   What is it?

BETSY   Helen, that's Hector saying that Geordie Clyne's on the road home from Weeck. He'll maybe have some word for us.

HELEN   Oh! *(She lays the clothes down on the kist and comes into the body of the room.)* Did ye see if he was on his own, Hector? Is there anybody with him?

HECTOR   I just saw the light, Helen. *(Looks out at the door.)* It's George right enough, though. Here he is now!

They wait expectantly as GEORGE'S *heavy footsteps are heard approaching. He comes in, a thick-set, taciturn man in his late forties, dressed in a similar fashion to Hector and carrying a lantern. He glances round the room, nodding silently to them all.*

BETSY   It's yourself, Geordie.

GEORGE *(with a faint smile)*   Aye, Bets. *(Goes to the table and lays the lantern down.)* I'm sorry I'm a bittie late — I had some trouble with the horse coming back.

He rubs his chin nervously as he talks, apparently unwilling to look at any of them.

BETSY *(taking his arm)*   Och, comeaye now and have a seat by the fire, George. Ye must be starving with the cold, boy! *(To* KEET.*)* Keet, get Geordie a dram, will ye?

KEET *goes to the dresser and pours out a large measure of*

whisky. BETSY *leads* GEORGE *to the rocking-chair. He sits down gratefully, rubbing his face with both hands.*

GEORGE Thank ye kindly, Bets. *(Sighs.)* The horse went lame on me no half a mile from Weeck and — oh, I've had the very dickens of a job to bring him home!

HECTOR *(impatiently)* Never mind the horse, George! We've all been waiting here! Have ye any word, boy?

GEORGE *(looks directly at* HECTOR*)* Aye, Hector. I've word.

BETSY *takes the dram from* KEET *and hands it to* GEORGE.

BETSY Now, take your time, Geordie.

GEORGE *takes the dram and nods.* BETSY *sits down opposite him.*

GEORGE Thank ye, Bets.

He takes off the dram in one go and, sighing, gazes into the fire, trying to find the right words.

HECTOR Well, come on, George! What is it?

BETSY *(hesitantly)* Ye've no . . . ye've no found the boat, have ye?

GEORGE Aye, Elizabeth. We found the boat. *(He glances sadly round the company, his voice beginning to break.)* Bits of it, anyway. We found the boat — and we found Donald Sinclair!

Of them all, only BETSY *realises the full import of what he has said. She turns away from him as if struck across the face and begins, slowly, to rise.*

BETSY *(softly, to herself)* Oh, my Lord!

She leaves the chair and begins to move, slowly, downstage.

HECTOR Donald Sinclair? What d'ye mean, ye found Donald Sinclair?

Concerned with BETSY, GEORGE *rises and moves towards her.*

GEORGE Donald's gone. *(Louder, forcing out the words.)*
   They've all gone!
HECTOR *(astounded)* What?

HECTOR *moves quickly to* GEORGE. KEET *begins to scream and*
HELEN *to cry out.*

KEET *(screaming)* No! No! No!
HELEN *(crying out)* Oh, dear God! Dear God!
HECTOR All gone? All dead? All my brothers?

Ignoring all about him, GEORGE *reaches out to* BETSY.

GEORGE Elizabeth . . .

BETSY *fights to control herself, he body tense and quivering.*
As she raises her anguished face heavenward, her clenched fists
rise almost as if of their own volition.

BETSY *(through gritted teeth)* David! David! *(She throws her*
   arms open and lets it all go in one tortured shout.) My
   Da-vid! ! !

SCENE TWO

The following Saturday, early in the evening. The funeral is
over, the mourners departed. The widows have tidied up and
take their places round the fire. A jug of whisky has been left
on the table, together with some glasses and a plate of scones.
BETSY *sits, motionlessly staring into the fire, on the rocking*
chair. KEET *sits on the stool and* HELEN *on the armchair next*
to BETSY. *On a chair she has taken from the table, sits* ANNIE,
a normally jolly woman of about thirty. CHRISSIE, *a few years*
younger, slim and emotional, sits at the table, quietly weeping.

29

ANNIE (*irritably*) Oh, Christina! For the love of the Lord, will ye stop that?

CHRISSIE I canna help it, Annie!

ANNIE Of course ye can help it! Get a hold on yourself, woman!

HELEN (*in reproof*) Annie! Please!

ANNIE Well, I'm sorry, Helen — but it's hardly the thing, is it? I mean, the minister said he might look in later on . . .

KEET Ach, what does it matter if he does?

ANNIE It matters a lot, Keet! What's the minister to think if the first he sees, as he walks through that door, is our Chrissie sitting there, cowning like a bairn?

KEET (*with cold hostility*) Likely that it's a natural thing for a woman that's lost her man.

ANNIE (*in like tone*) We've all lost our men, Keet — we've all got our grief! (*Pauses, sighs.*) D'ye think I dinna feel it and all? (*Shakes her head and rises ,turning away from them all.*) When I think of my Beel lying at the bottom of the ocean . . . Oh, I'll miss him! Sure, I'll miss him sorely! How could I no? I'll miss his jokes and his drinking and his . . . ach, I'll even miss his foul, nasty temper! I've had my share of weeping and — as God is my judge! — I canna think I've seen the end of it yet! (*Rounds on* CHRISSIE *severely.*) But I'm certain of this — I'll no put a lick of shame on my man's memory by making a fool of myself in front of strangers!

HELEN Och, Annie! The minister's hardly a stranger!

ANNIE (*contemptuously*) He's no got a drop of blood til a soul in the parish! A Cattach chiel, is he no? Belongs the south — Brora or someway! Huh! He'll no get a sight of my feelings, I'll tell ye that! Ye want to think shame on yourself, Chrissie! (*Sits down with yet another contemptuous glance at* CHRISSIE.) Robert wouldna thank ye for it, ye know!

As ANNIE *has been talking,* CHRISSIE *has pulled herself together, stopped crying and dried her eyes with a handkerchief which she now clutches in her hand as she addresses* ANNIE *with a quiet mixture of anger and pride.*

30

CHRISSIE Robert's past thanking anybody for anything, God rest him! And I'm past caring what ye or anybody else thinks of my tears, Annie! *(Draws herself up in her chair.)* All I know is, I've lost the kindest and bravest man that ever walked this earth — and I'd no be ashamed to weep an ocean for him or bother a dottle what anybody thought that saw me doing it!

CHRISSIE *turns quickly away.*

ANNIE *(irritated and slightly embarrassed)* Ach, ye! Ye and your oceans! What use is all this weeping and wailing, eh? Can ye tell me that? Atween the five of us here — and poor Maggie Sinclair that's at home in her bed — we've twenty-six bairns to clothe and feed and bring up decent! *(Shakes her head.)* We'll no do that by weeping oceans, Chrissie! We've a hard and bitter struggle ahead of us all — and, if we're to make a job of it, we better learn to leave our tears behind!

HELEN *(quietly)* Words and all, maybe.

ANNIE Eh?

HELEN *(with a smile)* Oh, I was just thinking, Annie. It's queer how it takes us all in different ways. *(Smiles to CHRISSIE.)* Some do nothing but weep and some *(turns to ANNIE)* do nothing but speak. *(Sighs and looks significantly at BETSY.)* And some just sit and do nothing at all!

BETSY *looks up, returns* HELEN'S *look expressionlessly, sighs and resumes her reverie.*

ANNIE What d'ye mean, Helen? *(Gives a sharp glance at BETSY.)* Ye're no saying . . .

Footsteps are heard approaching. KEET *hold up a hand for silence.*

KEET Wheesht! There's someone evennow!

Enter GEORGE, HECTOR *and* MARKIE, *all dressed in funeral blacks.* GEORGE *and* HECTOR *look distinctly uncomfortable in their suits, while* MARKIE, *a short and pudgy man in his mid-forties, seems as if he wears these clothes every day.*

MARKIE   Evening, lassies! How are ye all doing?

HELEN *rises and turns to greet them.*

HELEN   Oh, it's yourself, Markie! We thought it might be the minister!

MARKIE   The minister, is it? Hech, that'll be the day! I'm no often mistaken for the minister — eh, Hector?

HECTOR *(to* HELEN*)*   The minister winna be coming, Helen. He's off til Weeck.

HELEN   Weeck?

MARKIE   Aye, it's all been far too much for him, poor man. He's no all that strong when all's said and done.

HELEN   Well, I suppose . . . *(remembering her duty as a hostess.)* But here, dinna ye be standing at the door! Comeaye in at the fire, til I get ye a dram.

MARKIE *(jokily)*   By Jove, Helen, I thought ye'd never say!

HELEN *goes to the table and starts to pour glasses of whisky.* MARKIE *goes to the fire, warms his hands and stands with his back to it.* HECTOR *takes the chair that* HELEN *has vacated. Preoccupied with sadness,* GEORGE *sits down at the far end of the table.*

HELEN *(to George)*   Will ye be all right there, George? Ye're awful far from the fire!

GEORGE   Aye, Helen! I'm fine!

MARKIE *claps his hand together, rubs them vigorously.*

MARKIE   Well, well, well, then! And how are ye all keeping? Betsy?

32

BETSY *looks up at him, smiles faintly, then returns to her reverie.* MARKIE *shrugs and turns to* ANNIE.

MARKIE Annie?

ANNIE *folds her arms deliberately and turns away. Undeterred,* MARKIE *turns to* CHRISSIE.

MARKIE Chrissie? Yourself?
CHRISSIE *(softly)* I'm fine now, Markie.
MARKIE *(to* KEET) And how's Keetty?
KEET *(coldly)* How d'ye think?

HELEN *hands out whisky to the men,* GEORGE *first,* HECTOR *next and* MARKIE *last.*

HELEN Here ye are then, Markie.

HELEN *takes a seat, between* GEORGE *and* CHRISSIE, *at the table.*

MARKIE Thank ye kindly, Helen. I'd hardly think of going home til Weeck the night afore I had the chance of drinking til the memory of my old friends. Here's til them all! *(He toasts as the others murmur their assent.)* My, though, that was a grand bonnie kist ye got for Thomas, Helen! Eh? I'm no thinking that a kist like thon's been seen in Caithness this many a year!
HELEN Markie, I . . .
MARKIE Oh, I know, Helen, I know! He deserved the best and all — the fine, big chiel of him! *(Chuckles fondly.)* Goliath! We'll no see his like again for a while, I'll tell ye that! I mind once we . . . oh, by the way, Helen, is that a sconie ye've got there?
HELEN Oh, I'm sorry, Markie!

HELEN *picks up the plate and offers it to* MARKIE, *who takes a*

33

scone. She offers the plate to the others, but none of them are interested.

MARKIE I was going to say, I mind once — oh, years ago this, when we were all young — we were in Weeck for the herring. It was the year we had thon big fight with the Lewsachs, the Stornoway boys. *(To GEORGE.)* Ye'll mind on that, Geordie, will ye no?

GEORGE *(reluctantly)* Aye, Markie! I mind on it all right.

MARKIE Oh, a terrible business, thon! Just terrible! Started on the Saturday night and didna finish till the following Sabbath! They'd to get the troops in and all! *(Shakes his head.)* On the Wednesday, there were these Lewsachs — twelve of them there were — and they took it intil their heads that they were going to put Thomas Sutherland intil the harbour. *(Scoffs.)* They'd as much chance of doing that as they had of flying til the moon! *(Nods.)* One at a time he took them — by the belt, just — and slung *them* intil the harbour! Ye've never seen the like of it! A whiley after that . . .

HELEN Oh Markie, would ye stop talking about fighting, please? Ye know fine Thomas wouldna like it — he was never a violent man!

MARKIE Well, ye'll forgive me for saying so, I'm sure, Helen — but he never needed to be! Still, ye're right enough — he was a quate, peacable chiel, Thomas, would never worry any man that didna worry him. *(To ANNIE.)* It was your Beel, Annie, that was the lad for the fisticuffs!

ANNIE *(with hostility)* He was fit enough for ye, anyway, Markie Bremner!

MARKIE *(only slightly put out)* Oh, Annie! Beel never had any call to be fit enough for me, lassie! *(Reflects.)* And yet he was, of course he was — they all were! *(Laughs.)* It's lucky for me I had the brains and the sense to set myself up as a carter in Weeck — for I'd never have kept up with them chiels; Heroes, they were, every one of them! Heroes — and friends! I grew up with two of them and I knew the others all my days. *(Sighs.)* And now they're gone — all gone! *(Re-*

gains his good humour.) All except my old pal over there, Geordie Clyne. And, God knows, but I'm lucky to have him!

GEORGE *(growling)* Lucky? What d'ye mean, lucky?

MARKIE Well, George! I mean to say, boy, no blame til ye, but . . . well, if ye hadna slept in and missed the boat, ye might . . .

GEORGE *leaps angrily to his feet.*

GEORGE Ye've an awful big mouth, Markie! Ye want to watch that somebody doesna shut it for ye!

HECTOR *(restraining)* George! Steady, boy!

HELEN Oh, George! Please!

MARKIE Aye, George! There's no much point in losing your temper, man! Ye surely know I didna mean to upset ye, but . . . well, ye had a lucky escape, boy, and that's all about it. If ye'd been on that boat . . .

GEORGE *(angrily)* If I'd been on that boat, we might all have come home safe! *(His anger evaporates as he talks remorsefully, half to himself.)* The *Inflexible* was a man short. Another pair of hands might have made all the difference.

CHRISSIE Geordie, nobody can tell about that!

GEORGE No, Chrissie. Nobody can tell — and nobody can know. That's just the thing. I'll never know. *(Sighs.)* Until my dying day, I'll never know what *might* have happened if I hadna slept in — and missed the fishing.

GEORGE *sits down sadly.*

MARKIE Aye, it's a mystery right enough! *(By this time, he has finished his scone and he brushes the crumbs from his fingers, deciding that this is an opportune time to change the subject.)* Still! And what'll ye all do now, lassies? I mean, where are ye all going to go?

ANNIE Go? What in the world d'ye mean, man?

MARKIE Well, ye can hardly bide here, can ye? The land winna keep ye and the sea . . . well, ye'll never manage on your own.

35

HELEN It's a case of having to, Markie. Where else *can* we go?

The others chorus bewildered assent.

MARKIE But ye'll have this money from the fund, surely. That'll give ye a start . . .
ANNIE Money?
KEET Fund? What fund?

MARKIE *looks at them all in amazement.*

MARKIE The Calamity Fund they've started in Weeck for ye and the bairns! Dinna tell me ye've no heard of it!
HECTOR We've no had any word of such a thing, Markie!

The others, interested, murmur in agreement. MARKIE *goes to the table and lays down his empty glass.*

MARKIE Oh, have ye no? That's funny!
CHRISSIE What's it all about, Markie?
MARKIE Macadie and the Provost and one or two of the other big cheils in Weeck have got together to raise some money for ye. They've sent petitions all over the county and down south as far as Glasgow and Edinburgh — aye, even as far as London, itself. Mr Scott of Noss, I believe, was the one that started it — put in ten pounds! And the St. Fergus Lodge are having a concert in Weeck this very night! All the takings are to go to the Clyth Calamity Fund! I'm surprised ye didna know about this!
ANNIE *(in disgust)* Ach! It's charity, that's what it is!
HECTOR *(interested)* Well, it's maybe charity, Annie, but if folk want to give and they've a good heart about it . . . *(To* MARKIE.*)* Have ye any notion of how much they're likely to raise, Markie?
MARKIE Oh, I couldna tell about that, Hector. *(Pauses, thinking.)* Still, I have heard it said that a thousand pounds is possible.

36

This produces amazement from the others.

CHRISSIE A thousand pounds? Does that mean that we would get a thousand pounds?

MARKIE Well, no in your hand, Chrissie. That's no the way it's done.

HECTOR *(explaining)* There'd be an income.

MARKIE Aye, that's it, Hector. They'd put it by for ye, let ye have so much every week.

HELEN *(in awe)* A thousand pounds is an awful lot of money!

MARKIE Aye, but ye'll need it and all, Helen — every penny. If ye'll take my advice, ye'll put it til the best possible use.

ANNIE *(suspiciously)* And what would that be, Markie?

MARKIE Well, as I say, ye canna bide here. Ye'll need to move til surroundings that'll be a bit more comfortable — where the bairns would have a better chance. *(Pauses.)* Ye know, I've a feeling the best thing for ye all would be to sell all ye have to sell and move — lock, stock and barrel — intil Weeck.

KEET Weeck? *(In disgust.)* Och!

MARKIE Aye, Weeck. What's the matter with it?

CHRISSIE *(sceptically)* Oh, I don't know, Markie. I don't know if I'd like to live there.

ANNIE No more would I, Chrissie! Weeck's well enough named — a weecked placed if ever there was one! All that drinking and fighting and carrying on! *(With a sniff.)* No, no, my mannie! I wouldna like to bring my bairns up there!

HELEN Aye, but that's hardly it, Annie! *(To MARKIE.)* Markie, we're all country women here — we've lived all our lives on the croft. What in the world would we find to do in Weeck?

MARKIE *(with a shrug)* That would be up to yourselves, Helen — there's a lot of things ye could do in Weeck. I'm only offering advice, mind, but . . . well, ye might think of starting up a business. If ye all clubbed together, ye could easy manage . . . oh, a boarding-house, say, or a sweetie-shop . . .

ANNIE, HELEN *and* CHRISSIE *all make their reactions simultaneously.*

ANNIE *(derisive)* A sweetie-shop!

HELEN *(amused)* I've never been inside a boarding-house in my life!

CHRISSIE *(worried)* Oh, I'm no sure . . .

HECTOR *rises to intervene.*

HECTOR Now, just a minute, all of ye! Ye could all do a lot worse than to listen til what Markie says! *(Pauses.)* I know how ye all feel — and, Lord knows, I'd be the last to want to leave all that I've known and loved to go off til a strange place without the least idea of what's in front of me! But this much is plain; ye'll have to think of something. *(Shakes his head.)* Markie's right — ye canna bide here and be as ye were!

ANNIE How can ye no? Who says we canna?

HECTOR Och, Annie! Use your noddle, will ye no? It's a hard enough life ye've had here with your men beside ye — without them, it'll just be impossible! Ye'll never manage as ye are, without men to support ye!

KEET *gets up agrily.*

KEET Support us? What're ye talking about?

HECTOR Now, listen til me, Keet . . .

KEET No! Ye listen til me, Hector Sutherland! I'll do any job on the land as well as any man can do it — aye, and a good sight better than a whole dose I can think of!

ANNIE Good for ye, Keetty! That's telling him!

CHRISSIE *rises and turns on* HECTOR.

CHRISSIE *(angrily)* Aye, and I'll tell ye this and all! I'll manage a croft a lot handier than I'll manage a sweetie-shop!

HELEN *(equally angry)* Aye, Chrissie, or a boarding-house! *(Shakes her head.)* I wouldna have the first idea . . .

MARKIE *moves into the conflict.*

MARKIE Now, lassies! Will ye no listen for a minute . . .

ANNIE Och, ye shut your mouth, Markie Bremner! Ye've had far too much to say as it is!

HECTOR Och, for goodness sake, can I no say a word . . .

KEET I'm no caring what ye say, Hector! I'm no leaving here — no for all the money in the world!

HECTOR *(protesting)* But ye'll soon have no money at all if ye stop, Keet!

ANNIE What about this Calamity Fund, then?

HECTOR Och, that'll never do ye! It'll never make up for what my brothers earned! I'm telling ye — ye'll no be able to live!

CHRISSIE No be able to live! What d'ye think we're made of boy?

HECTOR Ye canna live on nothing, Chrissie!

HELEN But we'll no have nothing!

ANNIE Is that no just like a man? Twist everything! I'll tell ye this, Hector Sutherland . . .

MARKIE Oh Annie, for goodness sake . . .

The company has become very excited, except GEORGE, who watches silently, and BETSY, who decides that now is the time to speak.

BETSY All of ye, be quate! *(The very suddenness of her tone silences them. She rises and stretches her arms.)* Mind on where ye are, please! *(She moves slightly away from them, then turns to address them all.)* Markie, I want to thank ye, on behalf of all of us, for your kindness in coming back here this evening. We're sorry the minister wasna able to manage back with ye but . . . well, he offered up a fine prayer and gave us a bonnie reading afore he left for the cemetery. He's a good man, Mr Murray — be sure ye and give him our best if ye see him in Weeck. He's been a great comfort til us all these past days — and we're very grateful. *(Thoughtfully.)* Now, then! As far as this — what did ye call it again, Markie? Relief Fund, is it?

MARKIE Well, actually it's the Calamity Fund they call it, Betsy. The Clyth Calamity Fund.

BETSY   Calamity Fund it is, then. As far as the Clyth Calamity Fund's concerned, we're all glad to hear of it. (ANNIE *snorts and* BETSY *addresses the remainder of the sentence directly [and very severely] at her)* — and I say that without the slightest fear of contradiction! *(Pauses and addresses* MARKIE *once more.)* Atween the five of us here — and one other — we have twenty-seven bairns to clothe and feed and raise in the ways of the Lord. As if that wasna enough, there's Donald Sinclair's mother and father and his Auntie Isabel. They're all getting on now, and poor Donald was their only means of support — we canna let them down. So any money that's raised — however much it is — will be very welcome. We'll need every penny we can get.

MARKIE   Ah, Betsy! Trust ye to see the rights of it!

BETSY   Still and all, Markie, I think ye and Hector better understand something. We're no leaving this place — no for Weeck or anywhere else.

ANNIE   Well said, Bets!

HECTOR   Betsy, I thought ye of all people would see some sense. Good Lord, woman, can ye no see the croft'll never keep ye? Ye'll be far better off if ye . . .

BETSY   'Better off' is it? Huh, it's nothing to do with being 'better off', Hector. We canna leave the land and that's all about it! *(Looks about the room.)* This house ye're all standing in — we built it, ye know that. David and Thomas and Helen and myself, we built it — with our own bare hands! Helen and I hauled the stones from the burn and the shore — and our men put it all together to make this place!

HELEN   *(hushed)* Aye!

BETSY   The croft winna keep us, ye say? Good Lord, boy, was that no always the way? Why else do ye think our men went til the fishing? If it was money or comfort we were after, we might have left this place long since — gone off til Lybster or Weeck, where they're saying there's fortunes to be made. *(Shakes her head.)* I needna tell ye, Hector — it wasna for *that* that we've toiled here all these years *(Emotionally.)* Our men went til the sea so we could keep the land — keep it for ourselves and for the next generation and for the generation after that! Because this land is *our* land and we'll never give it up — no even if they come in here and put a torch till the roof of it! *(Lets her emotion go with a sigh.)* Oh, I daresay we would be 'better off' if we were to move til Weeck and open a shoppie or take in lodgers. But we canna. Our men — our brothers and our husbands and our lovers — died for this place, Hector. If we were to leave it now, they'd have died for nothing. We canna leave — and we winna leave. *(Suddenly weary, she turns away from them all.)* It's late. Helen, ye and Keet better go and get the bairns from their Grannie's.

HELEN   Right, Betsy. Comeaye, Keet.

Exit HELEN *and* KEET. ANNIE *and* CHRISSIE *exchange glances.*

CHRISSIE   Annie and I had better do the same, Betsy.
BETSY *(dismissively, without turning)*   Aye!

Exit ANNIE *and* CHRISSIE.

MARKIE   Well! I've a long road ahead of me . . . so . . .

BETSY *turns her head to smile at him.*

BETSY   Fine ye are then, Markie. Thanks again for coming.

Exit MARKIE. HECTOR *moves towards* BETSY.

HECTOR   Betsy, I . . .

BETSY *turns to face him.*

BETSY   Hector?
HECTOR   Ach, never mind! I'll see ye later on!

Exit HECTOR. *When he has gone,* GEORGE *rises slowly.*

41

GEORGE   Brave words, Elizabeth. But d'ye no think that there's something in what Hector says?

BETSY *(wearily)*   Och, Geordie!

GEORGE   It's all up til ye, ye know — if ye were to change your mind by the morn's morning, they'd all pack up and leave at your word.

BETSY   My mind's made up, George.

GEORGE *moves towards her quickly.*

GEORGE   Betsy, all I want to say is this — for as long as the Lord spares me, ye'll never want a friend in Geordie Clyne — whatever ye decide to do.

BETSY *(with a smile)*   Och, George! Did ye think I didna know that?

GEORGE   It'll be hard for ye, lassie. Harder than ye know.

BETSY   I winna leave — I canna leave. I owe it til David — and til all the rest of them.

GEORGE   Aye! *(He puts his hand on her shoulder for a moment, grips and releases it, turns slowly to leave.)* Well, God keep ye, lassie, God keep ye.

Although he is close to tears, GEORGE *seems reluctant to depart. He stops at the door.*

GEORGE   Mind now. Ye can always count on me.

BETSY *(quietly, in farewell)*   Aye.

On the point of leaving, GEORGE *suddenly bursts out emotionally.*

GEORGE   Oh, Betsy! What'll become of ye all? How will ye manage? How in the world will ye all survive?

Exit GEORGE. BETSY *walks slowly to the centre of the room.*

BETSY *(quietly, to herself)*   I don't know, George. I'm sure I just don't know. *(Pauses, very weary, drops her head. She takes a deep breath and, as she raises her head again, her eyes are blazing with determination.)* But we will! *(Almost savagely.)* I swear that til the Lord above! *(Emphatically.)* We *will* survive!

ACT TWO

SCENE ONE

Ten years later, early one evening in mid-August, 1886. Enter
GEORGE *with a fresh creel of peats. He goes to the fireplace,
sets down the creel and puts a couple of peats on the fire.
He hooks up the pot, then takes a seat on the rocking-chair.
He leans back, takes a pipe and a pouch of tobacco from his
pocket. He seems set to sit back and have a contented smoke.
When the sound of* HECTOR'S *voice off-stage makes him sit up.*

HECTOR *(off)* Fine then, Markie! I'll see ye later on, then.

Enter HECTOR, *carrying a kit-bag and a sea-chest.* GEORGE
leaps to his feet.

GEORGE *(surprised)* What . . . By Jove, Hector boy — is that
yourself?
HECTOR *(cheerily)* Hello, Geordie! How are ye?

GEORGE *puts his pipe away and goes to greet* HECTOR *warmly.*

GEORGE My, my, laddie! It's grand to see ye! It must be more
than a year since ye were here last!
HECTOR Two years, George. But I'm home at last — home for
good this time.
GEORGE D'ye tell me that? That's grand news! But comeaye,
laddie! Sit yourself down and let's have all your news! Ye'll
take a dram surely?

HECTOR *sits down on the armchair.*

HECTOR   Well, I might as well, eh? It's months now since I had the taste of real whisky.

GEORGE *goes to the dresser, chuckling.*

GEORGE   Aye, well — it's nothing but Geordie Fraser's best here, ye know!

HECTOR *(surprised)* Geordie Fraser? Is he going yet?

GEORGE   Geordie? Oh Aye! He was here shortago! *(Takes two glasses from the dresser and opens the jug of whisky.)* He's getting on, mind! The gauger nearly catched him once or twice last year!

HECTOR *(chuckling)* He'd have to be up early in the morning for that, if I know Geordie!

GEORGE   Aye!

HECTOR *smiles and looks round the room.*

HECTOR   Well, nothing seems to have changed here! Where are they all, George?

GEORGE *returns to the hearth with the whisky. He hands one glass to* HECTOR *and moves back to the rocking-chair.*

GEORGE   Och, all over the place, Hector! Ye've no idea what it's like nowadays, man! *(Resumes his seat.)* The women are all in Weeck — at the gutting.

HECTOR   Oh, of course! The season'll be well started by this time, I suppose?

GEORGE   Oh, Aye! Did ye no put in at Weeck, then?

HECTOR   No, no George! I put in at Liverpool — came up by road! Just got intil Lybster last night.

GEORGE   Oh, I see! *(Toasts.)* Well, here's til ye, boy!

HECTOR *(reciprocating)* And ye, George!

They drink.

GEORGE   And how's it all in the great wide world, then?

HECTOR   *(with a smile)*   Oh, they seem to be managing *(Thought-fully.)* Anyway, I've seen as much of it as I want. I've been fair taking long to be home for a while now.

GEORGE   *(with a sly smile)*   Aye, Keetty was saying she had a letter from ye.

HECTOR   *(smiling)*   Aye! *(More seriously.)* But how are they all managing? Is it still as hard for them, George?

GEORGE   *(with a sigh)*   Well, it gets better, Hector — it gets better. The years pass and the bairns grow and there's more hands to do the work, less mouths to feed. *(Brightening.)* Andrew's a great help, of course. He's a grown man now, ye know!

HECTOR   Aye, he'll be all of that! Where is he? Off at the fishing, I suppose?

GEORGE   Aye! In Weeck for the herring! I look at that laddie whiles and . . . ach, he's just his father all over again! David Sutherland til the life! *(Chuckles and has a thought.)* But here, ye didna see Janie when ye were in Lybster, did ye?

HECTOR   Janie? Ye mean wee Janie?

GEORGE   No so wee now, Hector! She's fifteen years old *(nods proudly)* and a student teacher!

HECTOR   Never! My, she must be clever, George.

GEORGE   It's her mother's brains she has, boy! Betsy was always the clever woman! She's done well, Janie — and all the others as well! They're all off in service or in Weeck or working on the land or at the fishing or someway or other, growing up, making their way in the world. *(Smiles philosophically.)* Time passes, Hector. It gets better.

HECTOR   Aye. I mind the night I stood here and told them they'd never manage without the men. They've no done so bad.

GEORGE   Looks like it! *(Finishes his drink.)*

HECTOR   And how about yourself, George? How're ye doing?

GEORGE   *(dismissively)*   Ach, just the usual, boy! I work my own place, do a bit of fishing — come round here once in a while and do two-three jobs that need doing. There's little enough I can do, but . . . well, I owe it til them, as ye know yourself!

HECTOR   I mind what a great help ye were in the first days. I'd have thought, by this time, that ye'd done enough.

GEORGE *(seriously)*   Oh, no, Hector! I'll never be able to do that!

There is a short pause. HECTOR *finishes his dram.*

HECTOR   It's been a long time now, George. What is it — ten years?

GEORGE   Ten years, seven months and two days.

HECTOR *(nods)*   And I suppose we're still no wiser of what really happened?

Thoughtfully, GEORGE *rises and goes to the dresser.*

GEORGE   A while ago, I ran intil Walter Murray. *(Turns to* HECTOR *enquiringly.)* Did ye ever know Walter?

HECTOR *(thinks)*   Walter Murray? *(Recollects.)* From Buckie? Plays the fiddle?

GEORGE *(nods)*   That's the man! We all fished together a couple of times on the West Coast — oh, years ago! He knew your brothers well.

HECTOR   Aye, I mind Walter fine myself! What about him?

GEORGE   He saw the *Inflexible* just before she went. He spoke til David.

HECTOR *(eagerly)*   Did he now? And was he able to tell ye anything?

GEORGE *(after a moment's hesitation)*   Only that David wasna at the tiller! ~~bar attached to rudder —~~

HECTOR *gets to his feet in surprise.*

HECTOR   What?

GEORGE *(nods)*   Aye, from what Walter said, it seems that Willie MacKay . . .

HECTOR *(amazed)*   Willie Mackay!

GEORGE *moves across the room as he talks.*

GEORGE *(bitterly)*   Willie MacKay! The youngest and least experienced man aboard was at the tiller. *And* they were carrying too heavy a sail! Walter shouted til them, but — ach, they either didna hear or they didna listen!

HECTOR   Willie MacKay! Good Lord, what in the world was David thinking of?

GEORGE   Hector, I know I needna tell ye what like your brother was. I knew David afore either of us could even walk. A wiser seaman never lived, but — by George! — when he got an idea intil his head, he was as hard to shift as the rocks on this coast!

HECTOR   Ay, George — but Willie MacKay . . .

GEORGE *(angrily)*   Men or boats, it was all the same til him! Put them to it and let the ocean make them or break them! *(With sarcasm.)* Willie MacKay would just have to learn! *(Bitterly.)* Well, I wonder if poor Willie's learned his lesson yet?

HECTOR *is at a loss for a reply to* GEORGE'S *bitterness.*

HECTOR   George, whether he has or no . . .

GEORGE *turns on* HECTOR *angrily.*

GEORGE   Dammit, Hector! If I'd been there, I'd never have let him do it! I'd have taken the tiller myself and brought her home!

HECTOR   George, it's all finished, boy! All over and done with! *(Helplessly.)* Ten years, George!

GEORGE   Aye! Ten years! For ten years I've had to stand by and watch these women work their fingers til the bone, break their backs nearly to bring their bairnies up! I sat at the side of Maggie Sinclair's bed and watched her die from the struggle.

49

D

I stood up there in that damned kirk at Bruan and listened til Murray — good man though he thinks he is — condemn Keetty in front of the whole congregation for a sin that was none of her own making! I've seen the bloom go from Helen's cheeks, watched Annie harden and Chrissie turn intil an old wifie afore her time! Worst of all, I've watched yon brave and bonnie woman, Elizabeth Sutherland, break herself, bit by bit, in the struggle to hold them all together! *(Pauses, suddenly aware of his emotion.)* Och, Hector! I'm sorry, boy. I didna mean to let it all spill out like that. This must be some homecoming for ye . . .

HECTOR *(comforting)* Och, never ye heed about me, George. *(Pauses.)* I know this — they'd all have had it a lot harder if it hadna been for yourself.

GEORGE Me? *(Shakes his head.)* All I've done is what I'm capable of, no more. Grannie Ellen — your own mother — she's done as much, taking the bairns so often and all. Markie Bremner's been good as well — he never comes out here, but he brings something extra. And there's been others that've given far more than I ever could.

HECTOR Ye've been a friend and a good neighbour, George. That's worth more than all the giving in the world.

Before GEORGE *can reply,* KEET *comes in, carrying two buckets of fish. Now twenty-nine years of age, she has lost her youthful gaucherie but none of her good looks. She wears a gutting apron, with a knife at the belt, and her fingers are bound with rags. She stops abruptly as she see* HECTOR, *who turns from* GEORGE *to smile at her. For a moment, they say nothing.*

HECTOR *(intimately)* Hello, Keet.

KEET *can hardly contain her delight. She puts down the buckets and runs to him. They grip hands.*

KEET *(ecstatic)* Oh! Oh! *(She breaks from him and goes to*

50

the door, calling off.) Betsy! Helen! Comeaye and see this! We've a visitor!

BETSY *and* HELEN *follow* KEET *in. Like* KEET, *they both look older* (BETSY *more so) and both are wearing gutting clothes.* BETSY *appears to be hobbling a little and* HELEN *is supporting her. Both are delighted at the sight of* HECTOR.

HELEN   It's Hector!
BETSY   Oh, Hector! *(To* HELEN.*)* Quick, Helen — run ye and catch Annie and Chrissie! They'll want to see him and all! *(Goes to.* HECTOR *with outstretched arms.)* Oh, Hector! How are ye, boy? How are ye?

Exit HELEN. BETSY *and* HECTOR *embrace as* KEET *looks delightedly on.*

HECTOR *(emotionally)*   Oh, glad to be home, Betsy — glad to be home!

BETSY *holds him at arm's length.*

BETSY   Let's take a look at ye, boy! Och, ye've hardly changed at all! What d'ye think, Keetty?
KEET *(happily)*   He's just the same as when he left!
BETSY   Comeaye and sit down, boy! Give us all your news.

As HECTOR *takes the armchair,* BETSY *hobbles over to the rocking-chair as* KEET *slips into the stool beside* HECTOR, GEORGE *approaches* BETSY *with concern.*

GEORGE   Betsy, what ails ye, lassie? Is there something wrong with your . . .
BETSY   Och, never ye be fussing me now, Geordie! I stumbled at the top of the road there and gave my foot a knock. Let me sit down and I'll be fine.
GEORGE *(uncertainly)*   Are ye sure, now?

BETSY *gives* GEORGE *a playful punch.*

BETSY Of course, I'm sure! *(To* HECTOR, *laughing.)* Geordie's like a mother till us all, Hector! Like an old clucking hen! Thinks we're all made of paper!

Huffily, GEORGE *goes to the table and sits down.*

GEORGE Well, somebody has to bother for ye — since ye'll never bother for yourself!

BETSY *signals her amusement to* HECTOR *behind* GEORGE'S *back and hobbles to the fireplace.*

BETSY And how's the great wide world been treating ye, Hector?

She takes the gutting knife from her belt and places it on the mantlepiece. She then takes off her gutting apron, folding it as they talk.

HECTOR Och, no so bad, Betsy. To tell ye the truth, I've no seen all that much of it.

KEET But ye were in Australia, were ye no? What like's that?

HECTOR Australia? Och, it's a bit like Thurso if ye want to know!

BETSY *puts the folded apron away in the kist.*

BETSY *(laughing)* Thurso! Och, Hector — surely never!

HECTOR For all I saw of it, Betsy, it might just as well have been Thurso! *(Amused.)* I went off til the navy three year ago to see the world — but it strikes me I'd have seen as much if I'd stopped at home!

Enter CHRISSIE, ANNIE *and* HELEN. ANNIE *carries a bucket of fish.*

CHRISSIE *(excited)* Where is he? Where is he?

HECTOR *stands up.*

HECTOR   Hello there, Chrissie!

CHRISSIE   Oh Hector!

She throws her arms about his neck and gives him a big kiss.

ANNIE   Lord bless me, Christina! Is that no just like ye? Any excuse to get your hands on a man!

CHRISSIE *and* HECTOR *break their embrace.*

CHRISSIE   Oh, Annie! He's lovely!

ANNIE   Oh, hush your mouth, Chrissie, afore ye make me blush for ye! *(Puts down the bucket and addresses* HECTOR.*)* So the prodigal's returned again, has he? Or the bad penny's turned up — whichever way ye want to look at it, eh?

HECTOR *(with good nature)* Ye've no changed anyway, Annie. How are ye?

ANNIE   Och, no so bad, boy! Barely managing, as usual! *(Gives him a quick, firm handshake.)* Good to see ye back.

HELEN *approaches* HECTOR *quietly and kisses him on the cheek.*

HELEN   Welcome home, Hector.

HECTOR   Thank ye, Helen.

BETSY   Och, Lord bless me, lassies! Do ye need to fash all about him there, like ye've never seen an unattached man in your lives afore this? Let the boyag sit down a minute and take his ease! How about a dram for him? Geordie, did ye give Hector a dram?

GEORGE   Aye, he's had a dram.

HECTOR *resumes his seat.*

HECTOR   To tell ye the truth, Betsy, I canna stop long. I've no been home yet, ye see.

ANNIE (*nudging* CHRISSIE) Oho, did ye hear that, Christina? He travels all this distance, yet he stops here afore he even goes to see his mother!

KEET (*icily*) Well, he could hardly pass the door, Annie!

ANNIE (*sarcastically*) Oh no, of course no! No after all the letters he's been sending til it this last year or so! No to mention all the scribbles he's been getting back — eh, Hector?

KEET (*snippily*) Well, at least he knows better than to write til your house, Annie Sutherland. All he'd get back from there'd be one big cross! (*Makes a sign with her finger to emphasise the point.*)

ANNIE (*offended*) Ye impudent limmer, ye! I'm as good at my letters as ye are, any day!

KEET Aye, but ye're no so great at minding your own business, are ye?

ANNIE Ye cheeky . . .

BETSY (*intervening sharply*) Annie, that's enough!

ANNIE (*appealing angrily*) But Betsy, she canna get away with . . .

BETSY (*emphatically*) Annie, I said that's enough! (ANNIE *submits to* BETSY'S *judgement silently.* BETSY *turns to* KEET.) As for ye, Keetty, when will ye ever learn to mind that tongue of yours? Could ye no see that Annie was only pulling your leg?

KEET Ach, she's always . . .

BETSY Be quate! (*As* KEET *obeys,* BETSY *turns to* HECTOR.) Ye see what I've to put up with, Hector? (*Sighs and shakes her head.*) Annie's right about one thing, though. It's no right that we should keep ye here afore your mother's had the chance to see ye.

HECTOR (*rises*) Oh, I was just in for a look, Betsy. I wanted to know how ye were all getting on. I'll be getting up the road now.

As BETSY *rises, she has a thought.*

BETSY   Here, there's a lockie fish there we brought home for your mother. You could maybe take it up til her, eh? Save Keetty a trail.

KEET   *(quickly)* No, it's all right, Betsy. I'll take it up myself. *(Explains to* HECTOR.*)* I've Willie to go for, in any case.

HECTOR   Your boy? He'll be getting big now, is he?

KEET   Oh aye! Intil everything!

HELEN   And how long will ye be stopping this time, Hector?

HECTOR   Oh, I'm home for good now, Helen. I've seen as much of the world as I want.

ANNIE   What'll ye do now ye're back, boy? Off til the fishing again, is it?

HECTOR   It's the only way I know of making a living — that and the land. It'll be a while afore I'm started, though. I've a new boat to buy and see about hiring a crew. That'll no be easy at this time of the year!

GEORGE   I've a man short evennow, Hector. Ye can come out with me for a bittie, if ye like.

HECTOR   Well, thanks George! That'll suit me fine! *(Pauses.)* Ye'll be going out the night, are ye?

GEORGE   Aye, later on. D'ye want to come?

HECTOR   Might as well, eh? Sooner I get started the better. *(Takes a breath.)* Well! I'd better be off now, eh!

He moves to pick up his luggage. KEET *joins him, picking up one of the buckets.* ANNIE, CHRISSIE *and* HELEN *group round them.*

BETSY   Dinna ye be a stranger now, Hector. Ye're always welcome in this house, boy!

ANNIE   *(with a nod to* KEET*)* I'm no thinking ye need worry about that, Bets!

CHRISSIE   *(poking* ANNIE *scoldingly)* Annie!

HECTOR   *(with a good-natured smile)* No, ye needna worry, Betsy. I'll be seeing ye later on, George.

GEORGE   Grand, that!

55

Exit HECTOR, ANNIE, CHRISSIE, KEET *and* HELEN, *chorusing their farewells.* GEORGE *rises and walks over to the door, watching them leave.* BETSY *rises and takes her gutting-knife from the mantlepiece. She is about to sit down again, when she gasps in pain. She grips her side with one hand (dropping the knife in the process) and holds on to the mantlepiece with the other.* GEORGE *goes to her quickly, taking her arms and supporting her.*

GEORGE *(concerned)* Betsy, are ye all right?

BETSY *holds on to him, a trifle giddy, but quickly recovers.*

BETSY Aye, George. I'm fine — just a wee bit tired, I suppose. Excited at seeing Hector.

GEORGE *helps her to sit.*

GEORGE Ye shouldna go til the gutting, ye know. Ye're no fit for it! Ye should . . . .

BETSY *indicates the fallen knife.*

BETSY Will ye hand me up my knife, please?

Displeased, GEORGE *picks up the knife and hands it to her.*

GEORGE It's no as if ye needed the money! The bairns are all grown, the worst is past ye . . .
BETSY *(sharply)* George, have ye no work to do, man?

GEORGE *pauses, offended.*

GEORGE Aye! I've work to do! I've business of my own to mind as well!

GEORGE *turns on his heel, about to storm out.* BETSY *regrets her words and calls after him.*

56

BETSY George! (GEORGE *stops, turns.*) I'm sorry, boy. It was wrong of me to speak like that — til ye of all people.

GEORGE *moves towards her.*

GEORGE Och, Elizabeth! Ye worry me, lassie — ye surely do. Trailing off til Weeck, gutting two barrels of herring and trailing back again — all in a single day! Ye're no fit for it, Bets.

BETSY It has to be done.

GEORGE Oh, what for? Ye've Andrew working for ye now — and all the rest of them . . .

BETSY *(with intensity)* For Janie! It has to be done for Janie.

GEORGE *(surprised)* Janie?

BETSY She's clever, George, ye know she is!

GEORGE Oh aye, but . . .

BETSY She's got more brains than all the rest of us put together. Life here is hard enough, I know — but I've had enough happiness no to want anything different for my other bairns. Janie though, she's special. The Lord has given her a gift and it's up til me — as her mother — to see that it's no wasted. *(Pauses.)* George, I want her to go til the University.

GEORGE The University! But she's a lassie!

BETSY *(sharply)* What difference does that make?

GEORGE *(equally sharply)* Ye know yourself what difference it makes! *(Pauses, milder.)* Oh Betsy, it's a hard road ye're asking the lassie to travel!

BETSY I didna say she was to have it easy — just different. Hard or no, she has to have her chance!

For a moment, GEORGE *doesn't know what to say.*

GEORGE *(angrily)* Betsy Sutherland, that's a whole dose of bloody nonsense ye've just given me!

BETSY *(shocked)* George!

GEORGE Ye're killing yourself with work so that Janie can go til the University, eh? Well, ye're killing yourself til no good

57

purpose! If Janie loses ye, there's no power on earth'll make here leave this place! As for the University . . . well, if that's what she wants, she'll manage it without your help. And d'ye want to know why? Because that lassie's nothing but her own mother all over again!

GEORGE *storms to the door as* HELEN *returns.*

HELEN George! What's up with ye, man?
GEORGE Och, nothing for ye to worry about, Helen! *(Points to* BETSY.*)* It's that damned foolish sister of yours!

Exit GEORGE. HELEN *turns enquiringly to* BETSY.

HELEN Betsy?
BETSY *(with a dismissive gesture)* Och, never heed, Helen. George is just being an old, clucking hen again!

BETSY *starts to cut the rags from her fingers and lay the strips out on her lap.*

HELEN Oh, poor Geordie! Ye'd think we were all his dochters the way he takes on! *(She undoes her apron and removes it, folding it up. She sits down on the armchair conversationally.)* Wait til I tell ye, though! I took a walk along the road with them — Keetty and Hector — but it wasna long afore they were letting me know that three was a crowd!
BETSY *(smiles)* Aye, I thought that was the way the wind was blowing!
HELEN *(delighted)* Oh, they'll make a grand couple! And it'll be grand to have a wedding again — we've no had one for years!
BETSY Chrissie's was the last.
HELEN *(with a sigh)* Chrissie and Robert! (Shakes her head *and begins to cut the rags from her own fingers. Both women work quickly, spreading out the stripes and winding them round the blades of their knives when they are finished.)* D'ye mind your own wedding, Betsy?

BETSY *(looks up with a smile)* Mind it? How could I forget it? It was the bravest day of my life!

HELEN *(giggles)* Well, ye worked hard enough for it, anyway!

BETSY *(in mock outrage)* Worked hard? What on earth d'ye mean by that, ye limmer?

HELEN *(laughing)* Och, ye needna pretend til me, Betsy Sutherland! I mind ye at the kirk at Bruan all these years ago, when we were lassies! *(Mimics.)* 'Oh David, is it no a grand day!' and 'What did ye think of the sermon, David?'

BETSY *(good-natured)* Och, ye were as bad yourself!

HELEN Oh, I was worse! *(Her laughter fades into a nostalgic smile.)* When I think of all the nights I'd lie awake in my bed, dreaming of him, wondering and worrying what in the world I could do just to get him to look at me! My Thomas! *(Rises and goes behind* BETSY, *gaily putting away her gutting clothes in the kist. She stops behind the rocking-chair, absently laying her hand on its back.)* Ye know, Betsy, for all the work and worry and hardship we've had these last ten years, I'm glad we didna shift! *(Dreamily.)* There's times I'll be cooking or washing or maybe just sitting by the fire and . . . oh, I feel close til him sometimes! That close that I feel that all I've to do is just look up and there he'll be — walking in at the door!

BETSY *sighs and leans back in the chair, joining her mood.*

BETSY Aye Helen! I know what ye mean!

For a moment, there is silence as they are both lost in their joint reverie. Heavy masculine footsteps are heard approaching, accompanied by a man's voice, quietly humming a tune to himself. For an instant, they think that the impossible has happened.

HELEN *(breathlessly)* Betsy! Who's that?

Enter MARKIE *cheerfully, carrying a large basket of groceries.*

59

He has hardly changed in the ten years since we saw him last.
At the sight of him, the women explode with relieved laughter.

MARKIE   Hello there, ladies! How are ye all the day? *(Puzzled by their laughter.)* What's the matter? Have I done something funny?

BETSY *(still laughing)*   No, no Markie! We're laughing at ourselves, no ye!

HELEN *Goes to* MARKIE *and takes the groceries from him.*

HELEN   I'm sorry, Markie — I'm afraid we're no ready for ye yet! We're newly back from Weeck, ye see!

MARKIE *sits down on the armchair.*

MARKIE *(dismissively)*   Och, that's all right, Helen! Never ye mind about me, I'm in no hurry. I'm stopping the night with my brother in any case — no going home until the morning. *(Has a thought.)* Here, I can give ye a lift til the gutting if ye like!

BETSY *rises.*

BETSY   That'll be handy, Markie. Thank ye kindly.

MARKIE *(dismissively)*   Ach, never mention it, Bets! It's no trouble.

BETSY   It's kind of ye for all that. Now, wait ye there evennow til I get your eggs for ye.

(Exit BETSY *to the right.* HELEN *puts the basket down on the dresser.*

MARKIE   And how does it suit ye having Hector back, Helen?

HELEN   Oh, it was grand to see him, Markie! He's home for good now, ye know.

MARKIE   Aye, I know. It was me that took him up from Lybster.

(Pauses with a sly smile.) And when's the wedding to be, then?

HELEN *(innocently)* Wedding? What wedding?

MARKIE Hector and Keetty, of course! What other wedding did ye think I meant?

HELEN *(amused, shaking her head)* Mercy me, Markie, there's no a lot gets past ye, is there?

MARKIE Och, the whole countryside knows about it, Helen. When Hector was home last, the pair of them were hardly apart. Folk in those parts arena stupid, ye know! *(With a contented sigh.)* My, though! Will it no be just grand to have Hector Sutherland back home again? The youngest of the Sutherland brothers and, as it turned out, the finest seaman of them all! I mind fine the night he brought the *Dauntless* intil Lybster — thon's a sight I'll . . .

HELEN *(abruptly, holding up a hand)* No, Markie! Please! I'm no wanting to hear ye on that!

MARKIE *(surprised by her change of mood)* But, Helen . . .

HELEN *goes to the dresser and opens a drawer. She takes a deep breath and turns to face him again.*

HELEN Oh, Markie! Ye and your story-telling! Ye always add arms and legs on til everything, d'ye know that? *(Goes to him, explaining.)* That night, four years ago, in Lybster's maybe worth a story til ye — but we dinna like to talk about it in this house. Ye see, in a queer sort of way, Hector's all we have left of our own men — and he's all the more dear til us for that. That night ye speak of, we nearly lost him . . .

MARKIE Aye, ye did that, Helen! How he managed it, I'll never know! He put the *Dauntless* on til the one part of the rocks where his crew'd have a chance. The boat was smashed intil smithereens — but every man-jack jumped clear!

HELEN *(nods)* The *Dauntless*. His pride and joy. I think that's what made him give it all up and go off til the Merchant Navy. It's a God's blessing he's come home safe. *(Before* MARKIE *can continue.)* So dinna ye be speaking of that night

— or any other wreck — in this house, Markie! It causes nothing but pain.

MARKIE *goes to her apologetically.*

MARKIE I'm sorry, Helen. I should know better by this time. I just feel inside myself that things like that should never be forgotten. *(With a self-depreciating shrug.)* Och, I'm a stupid old blether of a man!

HELEN *(forgiving him)* It's all right, Markie. We all know what ye're like. *(Brightening, she returns to the dresser.)* Anyway, it's all past us now! Hector's home again and going to marry Keetty. We're all together — together and safe at last!

There is a crash from off stage. Both react in alarm.

MARKIE What the . . .

HELEN *moves to the right exit.*

HELEN Oh, my Lord! *(Calling.)* Betsy! Betsy, are ye all right?

Exit HELEN *to the right, followed by* MARKIE. *Before* MARKIE *can leave, however,* HELEN *returns quickly.*

MARKIE Helen, what is it? Is Betsy . . .
HELEN *(urgently)* Run, Markie! Run for the doctor — quick!

Exit MARKIE *quickly, left. Exit* HELEN, *right.*

SCENE TWO

Early the following morning. Betsy is in bed, sound asleep. KEET *sits at the bedside, a cosy-covered teapot cradled in her lap. Enter* HELEN, *yawning and stretching, from the right. As she sees* KEET, *she smiles and nods towards the bed.*

HELEN *(quietly)* How is she?

KEET Sound. *(Rises and checks.)* I've your tea made.

KEET *goes to the table, puts the pot down and carries on to the dresser.* HELEN *goes and looks at* BETSY *in the bed. She turns again to* KEET.

HELEN Ye'll be stopping with her the day?

KEET *takes two bowls from the dresser, pours some milk into them from a jug, then returns to the table.*

KEET Oh, aye! *(Gives a concerned glance towards the bed.)* We'll need to take it in turns. The doctor says she'll be needing a lot of rest, and I canna think she'll be back in Weeck this season.

HELEN *moves to the table as* KEET *pours the tea.*

HELEN We'll work it out with Annie and Chrissie when they get here.

KEET Fine!

KEET *picks up one of the bowls, cradling it in her hands, and goes to sit on the armchair.* HELEN *picks up the other bowl in a similar way.*

HELEN Ye should take the chance of some sleep yourself now, Keetty.

KEET No, Helen — no yet. Hector and George'll be in shortly. — I'll wait for them. It's been a wild-like night and they'll be needing their breakfast. Markie's gone til meet them now.

HELEN *moves to the rocking-chair.*

HELEN Ye've seen Markie this morning, then? How is he?

KEET Aye, he was in here first light! Couldna sleep, poor soul! Wanted to know if there was anything he could do.

HELEN Ah, he's a good, kind soul, Markie — for all he's a blethering tongue on him! *(Glances towards the bed.)* There's nothing anyone can do — except maybe Betsy herself.

KEET *(nods)* Working too hard — sleeping and eating too little. That's what the doctor said.

HELEN Well, the rest'll surely do her good. I only hope she takes a lesson from this.

KEET *(laughing softly)* I doubt it!

KEET *leans back in the chair and closes her eyes.*

HELEN Ye're looking weary yourself, Keet. Are ye sure ye'd no like to lie down for a bittie?

KEET No, no, Helen! *(Smiles wearily.)* To tell ye truth, it's no that I'm no wanting it. It's just that . . . *(Half-dreamily.)* Oh, I just want to see Hector, that's all!

HELEN Ye're no worried for him, are ye?

KEET What? *(Realises what HELEN means.)* Och, no! *(She laughs and rises, almost brightly.)* The funny thing is, I'm sure I never will be! *(Moves towards the table.)* When Willie went . . . *(Sighs.)* Oh, but Willie was different! He was a crofter really — he never cared for the sea.

HELEN *(half to herself)* Aye, like Thomas!

KEET Hector's different. He's a fisherman — he belongs at the sea. *(Laughs.)* If the whole world was to turn til dry land, Hector'd be the most miserable man on it! Look at him now — no two minutes home and he's back at the fishing! So I'll never be worried for him. *(Drinks some more tea and smiles.)* I just want to see him come in, Helen, that's all! See him walk through that door in his working clothes, with the scales on him!

HELEN *(musing)* I know the feeling well, Keet. *(Pauses.)* And when d'ye think ye'll be married?

KEET Oh, I've no idea! We've no decided yet. *(Puts her bowl down on the table and goes to HELEN, extending her hand for HELEN'S bowl. HELEN hands it to her.)* I'll say this though — it canna come soon enough for me! *(They both laugh know-*

ingly and KEET *moves back to the table. She pours more tea from the pot.)* And did ye never think of getting married again yourself, Helen?

KEET *goes to the dresser for the milk.*

HELEN   Me? Oh no! We said it would be forever and . . . *(Laughs, slightly embarrassed.)* Ach, anyway, I never had the chance!

KEET *returns to the table, and milks the tea.* HELEN *rises and joins her.*

KEET   *(passing her her bowl)*   Och, come on, Helen! There's many a fine, swack man come marching up here . . .
HELEN   *(laughing and shaking her head)*   Och, none that was ever worth a second look, Keetty, none that I could ever compare with my own! *(Turns away from the table and takes a couple of steps towards the bed.)* Besides, with it all, these last years have been very, very happy — among the happiest years of my life. *(Pauses, turns to* KEET.*)* Och, it's maybe a wrong and wicked thing for me to say — but its true for all that! When the men were alive, they loved us well enough — and the Lord only knows we loved them! — but there was a man's place and there was a woman's place and ye had always to mind on it! Many's the night Betsy and I would be sitting at the fire there, mending or darning or doing some job or other, while the men would be sitting at the table here, drinking whisky and cracking away at this and that. It was fine and pleasant to watch them, but we could never join in.
KEET   Did ye ever want to join in? Men's things?
HELEN   No — but there'd have been ructions if we did! David and Thomas were the masters here, and Betsy and I just had to do what we were told! Och, I'm no saying that it was wrong or that I'd have had it any other way, only . . . well, they said we'd never manage, did they no? They'd have us

65

all in a sweetie-shop or a boarding-house in Weeck! Well, did we no show them, eh Keet? Ye and me and Betsy and Annie and Chrissie —we showed them they were wrong! It's been hard, but we've done it — we've managed to survive it all! And that makes me happy, Keet — happy and proud.

KEET *(smiles and nods towards the sleeping* BETSY*)* We'd never have done it without herself.

HELEN *(turns to look at* BETSY*)* No, God keep her! She's been our guide and leader through it all!

Enter ANNIE *and* CHRISSIE. ANNIE, *as usual, is sharp and brisk while* CHRISSIE *comes in with a kind of timid concern. Without a word to either* KEET *or* HELEN, ANNIE *strides over to the bedside and examines the sleeping* BETSY *critically.*

ANNIE How is she?

KEET *(irritated)* Wheesht, woman! She's sound asleep.

CHRISSIE Morning, Keet. Helen. What did the doctor say?

KEET *and* HELEN *resume their seats.*

HELEN Just that she's been overdoing it, Chrissie. She's to have plenty of rest and food — she'll be as right as rain in a couple of days.

CHRISSIE *takes a seat at the table.*

CHRISSIE Oh, thank the Lord for that!

ANNIE *takes the bedside chair and sits down next to* HELEN.

ANNIE Well, it's no me that likes to say it, but Betsy's brought this on herself, ye know! It's no been handy, the way she's been working lately!

KEET *(tartly)* Well, it gets to be a habit with some folk, Annie.

ANNIE *(sharply)* Eh? And what d'ye mean by that? Ye're no making out I dinna do my share?

HELEN (*quickly*) Oh, of course no! Keet meant nothing of the kind — did ye, Keet?

KEET Ye know what they say — if the glove fits, wear it!

ANNIE (*half-rising*) What? Ye cheeky limmer, dinna ye think that, just because ye've managed to capture a man for yourself, ye can be uppitty with me!

CHRISSIE Annie, will ye be quate, please? Ye and all, Keet. (*Glances towards the bed.*) If Betsy wakes up and finds ye at each other's throats, ye know fine what it'll be!

ANNIE (*mollified*) Aye. Well. (*Indicates* KEET.) She had no right to make out I'm lazy!

HELEN (*patiently*) Keet, will ye please tell Annie ye're sorry and that ye didna mean anything by that last remark.

KEET (*flatly*) I'm sorry, Annie. I didna mean anything by that last remark.

ANNIE (*unconvinced*) Ach, ye!

CHRISSIE And how are we to manage this, Helen? I mean, there'll have to be someone here with her, will there no?

HELEN Keet'll stop the day — she's been up all night in any case. I'll do it the morn.

CHRISSIE Fine! I'll do it the day after, then maybe Annie . . .

ANNIE Oh, surely! But I thought ye said she'd be fine again in a day or two, Helen?

HELEN Oh, likely she will! But we're no wanting this to happen again, are we? She'll no be back til Weeck afore the end of the season!

ANNIE Oh, I see! Well, in that case, would it no be better for the same person to look after her the whole time?

HELEN All right, then — but who?

ANNIE Well, I'd do it myself, Helen — but that would hardly be the thing. I mean, apart from the fact that Betsy and me would only fight like cat and dog, there's some people might think I'm dodging my share of the work! (KEET *snorts, but* ANNIE *goes on.*) I think it'd be best if it was one of ye in here. (*Hesitates.*) I think Keet should do it.

KEET (*surprised*) Me? Och, I'm no bothered — I'll do it and gladly, but — why me?

ANNIE (*roughly*) If Helen does it, she'll kill her with kindness. If Chrissie, Betsy'll only push her about — the Lord knows that's easy enough! — and give herself no rest whatsoever! But there's nobody'll push ye about, Keetty — as I know til my cost — and ye'll no be over-kind either! There's no doubt in my mind, Keet — Betsy'll be best off if ye look after her!

CHRISSIE (*amazed*) Lord bless me, are my ears deceiving me? Is that ye giving compliments til Keet, Annie?

ANNIE *rises, ignoring the last remark.*

ANNIE Is that settled, then?

HELEN What d'ye think, Keet?

KEET (*with a shrug*) Suits me.

ANNIE Right! Comeaye, the pair of ye! (*Moves to the door.*) The herring winna gut themselves!

CHRISSIE *follows* ANNIE *obediently.* HELEN *takes her gutting gear from the kist, and follows.*

HELEN I forgot to tell ye, Annie. We're getting a lift from Markie this morning.

ANNIE (*unconcerned*) Are we now? That'll be handy!

Exit ANNIE.

CHRISSIE (*as she goes out*) We'll be seeing ye later, Keet!

KEET Aye! Have a good day, all of ye!

HELEN Mind now that ye get some rest, Keetty!

KEET Aye, aye, as soon as I've seen the men in! Off ye go, now!

HELEN *follows* CHRISSIE *out.* KEET *goes to the door and watches them depart. As soon as they have gone, she turns wearily back into the body of the room.* BETSY *stirs, moving in the bed.*

BETSY (*half-awake*) Keet? Keetty? Is that ye, lassie?

68

KEET   Oh Dear!

KEET *moves quickly to the bed as* BETSY *sits up, rubbing her eyes.*

BETSY   Lord bless me, what time is it? *(Starts to get up.)* I'm needing to get ready for my work!

KEET *quickly restrains her.*

KEET   Now, now, Betsy — just ye stop where ye are! The doctor says ye've to stop in your bed for a day or two yet!
BETSY *(scornfully)* The doctor? Ach, what have I to do with doctors?

She tries to rise again. KEET *stops her once more.*

KEET   Behave yourself, Betsy! Do as ye're told!
BETSY *(sharply, but amused)* Eh? What's this, lassie? Are ye giving me orders in my own house?
KEET *(equally sharp)* That's it! Ye've been giving me orders all my life — it's my turn now! *(She sorts the bedclothes and makes* BETSY *comfortable.)* Now, then — would ye like some tea? There's a drop yet left in the pot.
BETSY *(still amused)* Thank ye, Keet. That'll be lovely!
KEET   Right ye are, then!

KEET *goes to the dresser, fills a fresh bowl with milk.*

BETSY   Where are the rest of them?
KEET   They're all off to meet Markie.
BETSY   Oh, of course! He'll be giving them a lift!

KEET *returns to the table and pours some tea into* BETSY'S *bowl.*

KEET   That's it!

69

BETSY Is that no just like the thing, eh? The one day I dinna need to walk — and I'm stopped off my work!

KEET *comes over with the tea.*

KEET Here, drink this and stop your moaning!

BETSY *smiles and takes the tea. She drinks deeply.*

BETSY *(contentedly)* Oh, that was grand! I had a awful drouth on me! I'm feeling a lot better now, Keetty, so I'll just . . .

BETSY *tries to rise again.*

KEET *(sharply)* Ye'll stop where ye are! Mercy me, woman, can ye no take a telling?

BETSY *sits back, resignedly.*

BETSY *(with mock pathos)* Oh, Keetty! It's the proper little tyrant ye are this morning!

KEET Well, it makes a change, does it no? How does it feel to be treated the way ye treat others?

BETSY *(giving in)* All right! All right! *(With authentic sharpness.)* And how long is this to last, eh? How long am I to be stuck in bed?

KEET A day or two yet. Even after that, ye'll need to take it easy. Ye'll no be back at the gutting this season.

BETSY *(protesting)* What? But, Keet . . .

KEET Betsy, no argument now! It's for your own good. We dinna want to lose ye.

BETSY Huh, I'll no be lost that easy! *(Pauses, sulkily.)* And what about yourself? Ye'll be losing money, will ye no, stopping at home all day?

KEET I'll manage.

BETSY Oh, of course! Ye're to be married shortly — or so they're saying!

KEET *(tartly)* Oh, d'ye tell me that? That's what they're saying, is it?

70

BETSY That's the story! *(Pauses.)* And what d'ye say yourself?

KEET *can contain herself no longer. She bursts out laughing.*

KEET Oh, Betsy! I canna wait!

BETSY *(happily)* Oh, ye limmer! What for did ye no tell me?

KEET How could I? He didna ask me til yesterday!

BETSY *(taking* KEET'S *hand)* Oh Keetty, I'm that happy for ye! Ye and Hector — who'd ever have thought it? *(Sadly.)* It's at times like this that I wish that David was still with us, to share the joy with me.

KEET Ye think of him yet, then?

BETSY Think of him? Lassie, I *burn* for him — there's no a minute of the day or night when I'm no longing for the touch of him! After all these years, there's no place colder for his absence than the bed I'm lying in now. *(Hesitates.)* Does it worry ye that Hector's at the sea so much?

KEET I've accepted it.

BETSY *(sharply)* Watch that, Keet!

KEET Eh?

BETSY Be careful what ye accept, lassie! *(Sighs and lies back.)* Oh, when ye're a woman, the world seems to expect ye to accept an awful lot! *(Smiles.)* D'ye mind what our mother used to say? 'Ye'll get what's laid out for ye, lassie!' *(Shakes her head.)* It's no true, Keet. There's times ye have to lay it out for yourself! *(Sighs.)* Oh, I daresay ye're right about Hector. If ever a man was made for the sea, it's him — and ye've no choice but to accept him for what he is. But acceptance in a woman is no virtue, Keet, whatever the world says! I'ts nothing more than a habit — and a bad, bad habit at that! So mind on what I tell ye, lassie. Never be too ready to accept! It's no worth it!

KEET *(fondly)* I'll mind, Betsy. *(Takes the bowl from Betsy, sharpens her tone.)* Now, there's one thing ye'll need to accept. The doctor says ye've to rest, so back under the blankets with ye . . .

BETSY *(irritably)* Och, the doctor! What does doctors know

71

about it? Besides, I've no had all the news yet! When's the wedding to be?

KEET Och, I'm no sure! Soon, though. We'll have to wait until ye're mended first!

BETSY *(dismissively)* Oh, that'll no be long! *(Smiles.)* So ye'll be a bride at last, Keet! Ye'll be looking forward til it?

KEET Hardly, Betsy — I'm long past that stage! But I am looking forward to having a man of my own — aye, and a house of my own as well!

BETSY And where will ye live? With Grannie Ellen?

KEET *(nods)* To begin with, anyway.

BETSY *(sceptically)* Ah well, in that case, I'd no be so sure about having a house of your own. She can be a stubborn old brute of a wifie, the same Grannie Ellen, as I know better than most! If ye'll take my advice, Keet, ye'll start as ye mean to go on! Take nothing from her! Ye mind that now! I know what I'm talking about!

KEET Och, Betsy! I can always . . .

BETSY *suddenly sits bolt upright in bed.*

BETSY Wheesht! What was that?

KEET Eh?

BETSY I thought I heard . . .

CHRISSIE *(off)* Keet! Keetty! . . .

KEET It's Chrissie! *(Puts down the bowl and moves to the door.)*

Enter CHRISSIE, *breathless.*

CHRISSIE Keetty! Get blankets! Quickly! Blankets and whisky!

CHRISSIE *moves into the room.* KEET *seizes her by the arm.*

KEET Chrissie! What is it?

CHRISSIE There's been an accident! Hector . . .

KEET *(alarmed)* Hector? What about Hector?

BETSY *throws back the covers and gets out of bed.*

BETSY Never heed evennow, Keet! Get the whisky! Chrissie, the blankets are in the kist!

MARKIE *(off)* Keep going, George, keep going! We're nearly there!

CHRISSIE *runs to the kist and takes out two blankets.* KEET *takes the jug of whisky from the dresser. Enter* MARKIE *and* GEORGE, *carrying an unconscious* HECTOR. *Both* GEORGE *and* HECTOR *are soaking wet and* HECTOR *has a long gash on his temple.*

MARKIE The table, Geordie! Quickly!

GEORGE *pushes* MARKIE *aside and lays* HECTOR *out on the table.* BETSY *takes a blanket from* CHRISSIE *and lays it over* HECTOR. KEET *comes forward with the whisky and* GEORGE *takes it from her.*

KEET *(confused)* Markie, what's happened?

ANNIE *and* HELEN *enter breathlessly.* GEORGE *props* HECTOR *up and tries to feed him whisky as* BETSY *tries to make him warm with the blanket.*

MARKIE *(quickly)* He was pitched overboard as they came in — struck his head on a rock! George had to go in after him! He was down for a long time!

CHRISSIE Oh, it was just terrible, Keetty!

GEORGE *(shouting, beginning to panic)* Oh, come on, Hector! Drink it, damn ye, drink it! *(The whisky is spilling over* HECTOR'S *face, having no effect.* GEORGE *hands the jug to* CHRISSIE *and starts slapping* HECTOR'S *cheeks.)* Come on, Hector! Come on!

MARKIE Ye'll never do it that way, George! Ye'll have to . . .

GEORGE *stops slapping and holds up his hand for quiet.*

GEORGE Be quate! All of ye, be quate! *(He puts his hand under the blanket, feeling for* HECTOR'S *heart. He lets* HECTOR *lie flat, throws off the blanket and listens with his ear. The others watch intensely as* GEORGE *finally groans.)* Oh, No! Lord, no! *(To* KEET, *shaking his head.)* I'm sorry, Keet. Hector's gone. He's done for!

GEORGE *turns away defeated.*

KEET *(in horror)* No! No!
MARKIE *(listening)* His heart's stopped. He's no living. Ye'll need to accept it, lassie . . .
KEET *(screaming)* No! *(Pushes* MARKIE *and* GEORGE *out of the way as she comes round the table.)* Out of my road! The sea's had one man from me — I'll be damned if she'll take another. *(She takes hold of* HECTOR *and starts to turn him over.)* Annie, help me! Helen, take his hands!

As ANNIE *and* HELEN *come forward and help,* BETSY *turns to* CHRISSIE.

BETSY His boots, Chrissie! Quick, now!

BETSY *and* CHRISSIE *pulls* HECTOR'S *boots off as* ANNIE *and* HELEN *start no chaff his hands.* KEET *hitches up her skirt and climbs on top of* HECTOR, *giving him artificial respiration.*

KEET *(as she works)* I'll no let him go! I'll be damned first!

The men watch in amazement.

CHRISSIE Oh, he's cold, he's cold, he's awful cold!
ANNIE Make him warm, Chrissie! Damn ye, make him warm!
HELEN Keep at it! Keep at it! Dinna lose him!
MARKIE *(encouraging)* That's it, lassies, that's it! Dinna stop!
BETSY *(tearing open her bodice)* Ach, your breists, women, your breists!

74

The others follow BETSY'S *example, tearing open their bodices and thrusting* HECTOR'S *freezing hands and feet into the warmth of their breasts. They clasp their arms around each limb and kneel as if in prayer.* KEET *pumps until she is exhausted.*

KEET *(repeatedly)* I'll no let ye go, Hector! I'll no let ye go! *(She collapses finally and slides from the table, still groaning these words. On her knees and almost weeping, she reaches forward and puts her hand on* HECTOR'S *cheek.)* Oh, Hector, Hector, Hector!

HECTOR *groans.*

KEET *(with hope)* Hector! *(She rises quickly.)*
MARKIE My God! He's alive!

HECTOR'S *body moves, disengages from the women's grasp. He pushes himself up on one side, half-conscious and exhausted, but alive.* CHRISSIE *picks up the whisky jug and* ANNIE *wraps the blanket round* HECTOR. GEORGE *takes the jug from* CHRISSIE *and starts to feed* HECTOR *some whisky.*

HECTOR *(dazed, coughing on the whisky)* Keetty — is that ye?
KEET *(weeping with joy)* Aye, Hector! I'm here!

MARKIE *comes forward, amazed.*

MARKIE I canna believe it! I canna believe it! If I hadna seen it with my own eyes . . .
GEORGE *(solemnly)* It's a miracle, just. A miracle.
BETSY *(calmly doing up her bodice)* No, George. No miracles. In this house, we've learned to live without such things. *(Claps her hands.)* Comeaye now, lassies — we'll put him til bed.

The four women carry the living body of HECTOR *out to the right. As* BETSY *follows,* MARKIE *pursues her.*

75

MARKIE How did ye do it, Betsy? What did ye do . . .

BETSY *(turning to him)* Do, Markie? We did nothing, boy! *(Indicates* GEORGE.*)* It was Geordie that went into the sea after him, Geordie that brought him home so quickly — it was Geordie that really saved him. *(Smiles.)* We did no more than what women have always had to do — we suffered and struggled and persevered. We persevered, Markie. That's all!

Exit BETSY. MARKIE *turns to* GEORGE, *still shaking his head in disbelief.* GEORGE *takes a thankful drink from the whisky jug.*

MARKIE I dinna understand this, Geordie. I dinna understand this at all!

GEORGE *laughs and hands the jug to* MARKIE. MARKIE *is affected by the release of tension signified by* GEORGE'S *laughter and begins to laugh too.*

GEORGE *(still laughing)* He's alive, boy! That's all ye need to understand! *(Joyously, shouting.)* He's alive!